Endeavor®

⑦

New Readers Press®
ProLiteracy's publishing division

The following teachers participated in pilot testing of Endeavor:

Evelyn Surma, Adult Education Teacher
Anaheim Union High School District, Anaheim, CA

Maria Pagnotta, ABE-GED Professor
Seminole Community College, Sanford, FL

Rachel M. Slavkin, Adjunct Faculty
Seminole Community College, Sanford, FL

Lora Zangari, Professional Development Coordinator
Lancaster Lebanon IU13, Lancaster, PA

Endeavor® 7
ISBN 978-1-56420-857-6

Proceeds from the sale of New Readers Press materials support professional
development, training, and technical assistance programs of ProLiteracy
that benefit local literacy programs in the U.S. and around the globe.

Contributing Author: Vista Resources, Inc.
Developmental Editors: Ellen Northcutt, Donna Townsend
Creative Director: Andrea Woodbury
Production Specialist: Maryellen Casey
Art and Design Supervisor: James P. Wallace
Illustrator: Wendy Rasmussen, represented by Wilkinson Studios, Inc.

Contents

You Can Save Your Own Life

Learning Objectives

In this lesson you will:

- Learn about signs that mean you should see a doctor.

- Identify fact and opinion.

- Master the key vocabulary used in the article.

- Write about what it means to you to take responsibility for your own health.

Key Vocabulary

confused *(adjective)* feeling uncertain or unclear

decipher *(verb)* to make out the meaning of something that is unclear

digestion *(noun)* the ability of the body to turn food into energy

depression *(noun)* a mental illness that causes feelings of sadness and hopelessness

hesitate *(verb)* to pause or hold back

internal *(adjective)* inside

permanent *(adjective)* continuing without change

reluctance *(noun)* feeling or showing that you don't want to do something

spasm *(noun)* a sudden violent movement of the muscles

symptoms *(noun)* the signs of illness

Before You Read

As you read the beginning of this article, you know it will be about health, and the signs that show you may have health problems. Begin by asking yourself an active reading question: What do I want to get out of this reading? You can also summarize each section of the article. These active reading strategies can help you understand and focus as you read.

Ask yourself questions.

1. What signs are the most important to watch out for?

_____

_____

_____

_____

_____

_____

2. Should I visit the emergency room or my doctor if I have these signs?

_____

_____

_____

_____

_____

_____

Summarize.

After you read a section of the story, try summarizing what happened in that section. In your own words, briefly tell what happened.

Signs You Can't Ignore

Knowing the signs of serious illnesses can save your life. Read on to find out what to worry about—and what not to.

You have a headache. Your stomach hurts. You are losing weight. These symptoms could mean nothing—or they could be signs that something is seriously wrong with your health. You might **hesitate** to go to the doctor when you think something is wrong. You might not want to take up the doctor's time if you aren't really sick. You might not be covered by insurance and fear you won't be able to pay the bills. Those are all reasonable concerns. For some **symptoms,** though, you need to break through your **reluctance** and visit the doctor. Here are some signs you should not ignore.

Weight loss or loss of appetite

If you are on a diet and lose weight, good for you. But if you are not on a diet, and you experience weight loss, take note. Sudden or unexpected weight loss can signal several serious medical problems. AIDS or cancer, for example, may lead to weight loss and tiredness. Unexplained weight loss can also be caused by **depression.** When people are depressed, they often lose interest in eating.

Stomach pain

You have probably experienced the kind of stomach pain that comes after you eat something that doesn't agree with you. That kind of pain is usually nothing to worry about. However, if you have stomach pain that lasts several months, see a doctor. You should also see a doctor if the pain is so bad that you can hardly move or if you can't eat without throwing up. Possible causes for these symptoms include cancer or other serious problems with your **internal** organs, such as your stomach, liver, or intestines.

1. Why would someone hesitate to go to the doctor?

_____

2. Facts can be proven. Opinions are what the writer feels. Find an example of a fact and an example of an opinion in the section you just read.

_____

_____

In the next section, you will learn about more symptoms to be concerned about. Underline or highlight what conditions they might signal.

Headache

25 We all get headaches, and headaches are no fun. When it comes to deciding if a headache is serious enough to see a doctor, you should trust yourself. You will know if a headache is different from the usual headaches you get. It might be the worst headache you've ever had. It might be a headache that lasts for days, and nothing gives you relief.

30 If you take medicine for high blood pressure, an unusually severe headache might mean you have an aneurysm , a weak spot in an artery wall that can burst and kill you. If you have a stiff neck along with your headache, it may mean that you have meningitis , a serious infection.

If you have any of those kinds of headaches, you need to see your doctor.

Black stools

35 The food you eat affects the color of your stools, but despite what some people might have told you, black stools are not caused by eating black beans. If you notice that your stools are very black, you should make an appointment with your doctor. You could have bleeding problems or cancer. It may be difficult to talk about stools, but it's a lot more difficult to deal with cancer.

40 ### Chest pain

Chest pain can be a difficult symptom to **decipher.** If you have chest pain when you move your arm forward or backward, you might just have a pulled muscle. If you are under a lot of stress, you might feel a twisting pain, or **spasm,** in your chest. This may be a sign that you are having a panic attack

45 which is not a serious health problem. Or it might mean that you are having problems with your **digestion.** If you are not sure and you want to be safe, see a doctor.

Chest pain could also mean that you are having a heart attack. If you have shortness of breath along with chest pain, you may have a blood clot in your

50 lungs. This can be dangerous, and you should see a doctor immediately.

aneurysm (noun)
a weakening of the wall of a blood vessel

meningitis (noun)
an infection of the brain

clot (noun)
a lump of thick blood

3. When should you go to the doctor for a headache?

_____

4. Which chest pains are usually not serious problems?

_____

There is one guideline that covers most questions about whether or not to see a doctor. Continue reading to find out what that guideline is. When you find it, mark it in the margin.

Stroke signs

Strokes aren't just for old people. Young people can have them, too. Some young people who have strokes are just unlucky. But people who smoke are more likely to have a stroke no matter how old they are.

55   A stroke happens in your brain, most commonly from a blood clot. The clot keeps blood from getting to your brain, and can cause **permanent** damage or death.

Here, doctors say, are some of the signs of a stroke. You may feel **confused** or notice that you slur your speech. You may also notice that although you

60   are trying to talk, sounds come out instead of words. If you look in the mirror, one side of your face might be sagging. That's paralysis . You may experience paralysis on one side of your face or on one side of your body. Other signs of a stroke include burning pains and a tingling feeling on one side of your body.

If you recognize any of these things happening to you, act immediately.

65   You should get to an emergency center as quickly as possible. Call 911 for an ambulance. If doctors are able to treat you for a stroke right away, you may be able to recover completely. Early treatment can keep you from having permanent brain damage. Early treatment can save your life.

Just as important as these general guidelines for seeing a doctor is what your

70   gut tells you. You are smart. You know when something is not right in your body. When you feel that way, you should see a doctor. If you go to the doctor and find out that nothing is wrong with you, you may feel mildly embarrassed. But if you really are sick, you could be saving your own life.

slur (verb)
   to pronounce words in a way that is difficult to understand

paralysis (noun)
   the loss of the ability to move

5. What is a stroke?

_____

6. What should you do if you think you are having a stroke?

_____

After You Read

Build a robust vocabulary.

Writing Sentences   Write a complete sentence to respond to each of the following questions or statements. Use the underlined word in your answer. Use the definitions on page 5 to help you.

1.   Name an <u>internal</u> organ.

   _____

2.   Name two <u>symptoms</u> of a stroke.

   _____

3.   What is a sign of <u>depression</u>?

   _____

4.   When might you <u>hesitate</u> before speaking?

   _____

5.   Tell about a time when you felt <u>confused</u>.

   _____

Sentence Completions   Complete each sentence using a word from the box.

confused	decipher	digestion	depression	hesitate
internal	permanent	reluctance	spasm	symptoms

1.   Tom lifted something heavy and felt a _____ twist up his back.

2.   Holly had a terrible headache, but she felt _____ about visiting her doctor.

3.   Not dealing with a stroke right away may lead to _____ problems you live with for the rest of your life.

4.   Claudia felt dizzy and thirsty, and wasn't sure how to _____ her symptoms.

5.   Gary had stomachaches and other problems with _____ .

Word Building   A **root word** is a base word that other words are made from. For example, you can make *books, bookish, booking,* and *rebook* from the root word *book.*

Look at the words below and underline the root word. Check your answers with a partner.

preheat	forgetful	foolish	stapler	unwise

-ing	-ful	pre-	re-

Use the sets of letters in the box to make new words. Write sentences that use the new words.

1. use: _____

2. join: _____

3. sleep: _____

4. view: _____

5. help: _____

TIP: Look for the root word within words you don't know. That may help you decide the meaning of the word. For example, if you know the word *master,* you might be able to tell that *masterful* means "acting like a master."

Writing Activity   Write a short paragraph that correctly uses key vocabulary words to tell why some medical problems should not be ignored. Use at least four of the words from the list on page 5. Reread the definitions, if necessary.

_____

_____

_____

_____

Think about your reading.

Check your comprehension.   Answer each question. If you don't know the answer, reread the lines in parentheses.

1. What can be causes of sudden weight loss? (lines 12–14)

_____

2. When should stomach pain be a reason to see a doctor? (lines 18–20)

_____

3. Why should you see a doctor if you have a headache and a stiff neck? (lines 29–32)

_____

4. What are the signs of a stroke? (lines 58–63)

_____

Use reading skills: Identify fact and opinion.

Writers often mix fact and opinion. A **fact** is something that can be proven. *There are 50 states in the United States* is a fact. *The state of Idaho has the best potatoes* is an **opinion.** When you read, keep alert so you don't mistake the writer's opinions for facts.

Identify fact and opinion.   In the first paragraph of the article, you read *Those are all reasonable concerns.* That is the writer's opinion. A fact on the same issue might be, *Some people say they don't go to doctors because they can't afford the cost.*

Reread these sentences from the article.

> If you notice that your stools are very black, you should make an appointment with your doctor. You could have bleeding problems or cancer. It may be difficult to talk about stools, but it's a lot more difficult to deal with cancer.

1.   What is the fact in these sentences?

   Fact: _____

2.   What is the opinion in these sentences?

   Opinion: _____

Use a graphic organizer.

You can use a graphic organizer like the one below to help you separate fact from opinion. Reread the second section of the article. Fill in this chart with three opinions and three facts from that section.

Fact	Opinion

Write About It

Write your opinion.

What does it mean to you to take responsibility for your own health? When you write your opinion, you state what you think about something. Write a paragraph that tells what you think a person who takes responsibility for his or her own health does. Be sure to include facts to back up your opinion. You can use the information you learned in this article to help you make your points.

Prewriting   The main idea of your paragraph is to explain what taking responsibility for your own health means to you. Use this web to write down points that support your opinion. You may need more or fewer ovals to write the information.

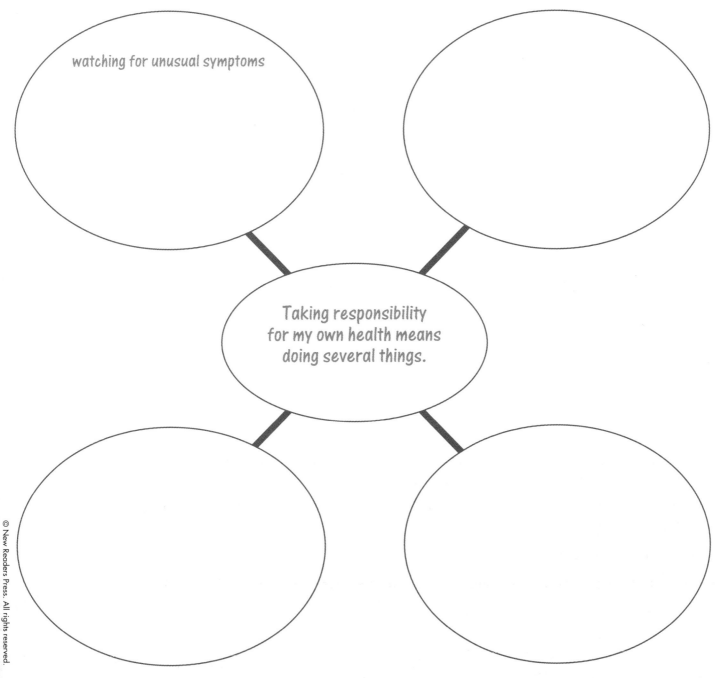

watching for unusual symptoms

Taking responsibility for my own health means doing several things.

Thinking Beyond Reading   Discuss your paragraph with a partner. Compare graphic organizers and add ideas as you talk. You can also talk about these questions.

- What responsibility do people have to pay attention to their health?

- What should people do if they don't have a doctor?

- What should people do if they don't have money for a doctor?

Write a draft.   Write a first draft of your paragraph. You might begin like this: "I think I have a responsibility to myself and to my family to stay healthy. Luckily, there are things I can do." Use the information in your graphic organizer to help you.

_____

_____

_____

_____

_____

_____

_____

_____

_____

_____

_____

_____

_____

_____

_____

Revise and create a final draft.   Write your final draft on a separate piece of paper. As you revise, check your draft for these specific points:

- Did you tell what your opinion is about your responsibility for staying healthy, and why you have that opinion?

- Did you write ways you can stay healthy?

- Did you check spelling and grammar to make sure your writing is clear and correct?

Getting Along at Work

Learning Objectives

In this lesson you will:

▨ Read a story about a person dealing with a difficult boss.

▨ Make judgments about what you read.

▨ Master the key vocabulary used in the story.

▨ Write a paragraph that summarizes the story.

Key Vocabulary

caressed *(verb)* touched in a tender, loving way

efficient *(adjective)* doing well without wasting time or energy

frustration *(noun)* a feeling that something is stopping you from doing something

ingratiating *(adjective)* intending to gain someone's favor; pleasing

insincerity *(noun)* fake feeling

maneuvering *(verb)* moving in a skillful way

sarcastically *(adverb)* in a way that is meant to hurt or make fun of someone

stifled *(verb)* held back or stopped

truce *(noun)* a temporary agreement to stop fighting

urgent *(adjective)* calling for very quick attention

Before You Read

From the title of the story, you know you will be reading about someone's problems at work. As an active reader, begin by thinking about what you already know about bosses and work. Then, as you read the story, keep predicting what might happen next.

Use what you know.

THINK ABOUT IT

1. What are some things you have done or someone you know has done when you had a difficult boss?

   _____

   _____

   _____

I'm thinking about a bad boss I've had and bad bosses I've heard about. What's funny is that they were upsetting in different ways, but they all made your life miserable.

2. What happened when you tried different ways to deal with a difficult boss?

   _____

   _____

   _____

Predict what will happen.

THINK ABOUT IT

1. Read the title of the story and look at the illustration. What do they tell you?

   _____

   _____

   _____

When I had a terrible boss, I hated my job and wanted to leave. I wonder if Al will feel like this, too.

2. Al's problem at work seems to be a bad boss. What do you think might make the boss a bad one?

   _____

   _____

   _____

An Awful Boss

Al's stuck in a job he likes with a boss he hates. What should he do? What would *you* do? Use sticky notes to jot down what you think about Al's situation.

Al slumped in his chair, took off his hat, and rubbed his hair. "I'm telling you, Tami, the guy hates me. I don't know what I did to him, but it's ridiculous. He watches me like a hawk, and when I do anything wrong, the smallest thing, he gets on my back. He doesn't do it to anyone else. I've had it."

5 "Al—we need this job." Tami's voice was soft in his ear. She trailed her fingers up and down his arm. "It's a good job. It's got good benefits ." Tami's voice got more **urgent.** "Al—we're going to have a baby! You can't just quit. Stick it out. Come on, honey." Her voice **caressed** him.

Al sighed. Tami had quit her job in a beauty salon, scared that the fumes 10 from the hair dye and other products would hurt the baby. Now they were living just on his salary, not exactly Bill Gates wages. And with his boss Steve on him all the time, Al wasn't sure how much longer he could take it.

"The thing is, it's not like I do a bad job or anything. I'm the youngest guy there, by a lot, but I do the work. I do a good job. But I hear you, Tami. I'll 15 think of something," he said. If I could just figure out what, Al thought.

The next day, Al walked in with the attitude that whatever his lousy boss said, he wouldn't bite. The abuse started right away. "Nice of you to join us," his boss Steve said **sarcastically,** even though Al was right on time. Al smiled briefly and went to his forklift. Then he shook his head. "What's that about?" 20 Steve yelled. "You got a problem with me? With being on time?"

Al paused to gather himself for a second. He **stifled** the urge he had to taunt Steve back. "I was on time, and you know it," Al said evenly, his voice

benefits *(noun)*
 things that you get,
 in addition to money,
 from your job

tight. "Sorry if I seemed to be disrespectful." The rest of the day, both Steve and Al stayed clear of each other.

1. What would you do if your boss greeted you in the morning the way Steve greeted Al?

   _____

2. Do you think Tami should have quit her job in the beauty salon? Explain.

   _____

3. Do you think Al should keep his job for the benefits? Explain.

   _____

Al's problems with Steve don't seem to be over. Underline sentences in the next part of the story that tell what causes the next blowup.

pallet (noun)
> a platform that holds goods and can be moved around

merchandise (noun)
> goods for sale

spreadsheet (noun)
> a chart with information in rows and columns

25   For a while, the **truce** held. Steve ignored Al, and Al smiled politely at Steve and did his work as carefully as he could. There was a lot to keep track of—which pallets belonged in which rows in the huge warehouse, where merchandise was kept, where to record in the huge spreadsheet every movement of goods. Al did like the work, though. He liked being **efficient** with
30   the huge forklift, **maneuvering** it carefully in tight spaces. It was a satisfying job.

Al was beginning to relax at work. Steve hadn't been able to find anything in Al's performance to complain about, although he did glare darkly at Al sometimes when Al's **ingratiating** smile seemed less than sincere. Al didn't care. He'd made peace with Steve, deciding that if a little **insincerity** would
35   make his job secure, he was fine with it.

Then one day, things went sour at work. Al hadn't seen a pile of goods to the left of the forklift. He hit it with the side of the lift and the pile toppled. Steve was there like a shot. "You moron," Steve yelled. Al could tell Steve was enjoying the opportunity to finally provoke Al. "Too dumb to work a forklift!
40   You oughta be fired, moron."

Al's face colored. He angrily opened his mouth, and then he thought of Tami's face and took a deep breath. "I'll try harder," he said through gritted teeth. Steve looked at him sharply. Then he walked away.

Al fumed until he got home. Then all the **frustration** of the day came out.
45   Al threw a chair across the room. "Calling me a moron! *He's* a moron! Tami, I can't take it! The guy is out to get me." Tami just looked at him sadly.

4. Why do you think Steve and Al finally provoke each other again?

   _____

5. Do you think Al was right to tell Steve he'd try harder? Why?

_____

Think about what you might do in Al's place. Write on a sticky note what you think Al will do. Then read on to find out what happens. Add a star to the sticky note if you found that your prediction was right. Write an X on the sticky note if your prediction was not right.

The next day at work, Al was still fuming. Al glared at Steve. Al glared at everyone. Finally, Ben took him aside. Ben was an old, grizzled guy who had worked there for years and had the attitude of a man who'd seen it all.

50   "Listen, Al," he said, "there're some things you need to know. Steve had a younger brother. They were really close. His brother was about your age when he died in a car accident a couple of years ago. I think Steve still misses him. I think he looks at you and gets angry when he realizes that you're alive and his brother isn't. Really, there isn't anything else I can think of. You do a

55   good job."

"What am I supposed to do?" Al said miserably. "Kill myself?"

Ben said, "OK, this may seem ridiculous, but what if you tell him you know about Stan and you're sorry, but there's nothing you can do about it?"

"He'll fire me," Al said.

60   "Maybe. Probably not. But either way, can you stand this much more?"

Good point, Al thought. Right after work, he worked up his courage and approached Steve. "Listen," Al said nervously. "Can I talk to you?"

Steve's eyes narrowed. He nodded quickly.

Al took a deep breath. "I know about your younger brother who was killed."

65   "Who told you?" Steve said sharply.

"Doesn't matter," Al said. "But you know I do a good job. And you know I can't do anything about your brother, right?"

Steve didn't say anything, so Al kept talking. About brothers, and losing people, and families. He told Steve about the baby coming, and Tami. Finally,

70   Steve cracked a small smile. He said, "I gotta go home, Al." Then he laid a hand briefly on Al's back. "But you're OK. Yeah, you're OK."

Yeah, thought Al, feeling happy for the first time in days, yeah, I am OK.

6. Do you think Ben gave Al good advice? Why do you think so?

_____

7. Did Al do the right thing when he talked to Steve about his brother? Why do you think so?

_____

After You Read

Build a robust vocabulary.

Writing Sentences   Write a complete sentence to respond to each of the following questions or statements. Use the underlined word in your answer. Use the definitions on page 15 to help you.

1. What is something that makes you feel <u>frustration</u>?

   _____

2. What is an example of <u>insincerity</u>?

   _____

3. Name a time when two people might call a <u>truce</u>.

   _____

4. Tell when you <u>stifled</u> something you wanted to say.

   _____

5. What is something that needs <u>urgent</u> action?

   _____

Sentence Completions   Complete each sentence using a word from the box.

caressed	efficient	frustration	ingratiating	insincerity
maneuvering	sarcastically	stifled	truce	urgent

1. "Oh, sure," Kayla said _____ when she didn't agree.

2. Brian enjoyed _____ the truck through the small spaces in the brickyard.

3. When Bob _____ his wife's arm, she smiled.

4. Hal's _____ smile seemed totally fake.

5. Kelli was so _____ doing her work that she finished two hours early.

Word Building   A **prefix** is a group of letters added to the beginning of a word. When a prefix is added, a new word with a new meaning is formed. For example, you know the prefix *un-* means "not" in the word *unhappy.* Here are some other prefixes, their meanings, and sample words. The prefix *micro-* means "small" in the word *microscope, non-* means "not" in the word *nonsense,* and *under-* means "below" in the word *underground.*

Circle the prefix in each word. Check your answers with a partner.

underwear	nondairy	microsurgery	undercover

Add *micro-, non-,* or *under-* to each word below. Then use the new word in a sentence.

1. phone: _____

_____

2. alcoholic: _____

_____

3. cover: _____

_____

4. age: _____

_____

5. sense: _____

_____

TIP: If a word is long and you notice a prefix at the beginning, take the word apart. Look at both the prefix and the base word to see if you can figure out the meaning of the word.

Writing Activity Write a short paragraph that correctly uses key vocabulary words to give advice about dealing with a difficult boss. Use at least four of the words from the list on page 15. Reread the definitions, if necessary.

_____

_____

_____

Think about your reading.

Check your comprehension. Answer each question. If you don't know the answer, reread the lines in parentheses.

1. Why does Al dislike his boss? (lines 1–4)

_____

2. How does Al respond when Steve yells at him for knocking over a pile of goods at work? (lines 41–43)

_____

3. Who is Ben? (lines 48–49)

_____

4. Why is Al happy at the end of the story? (lines 70–72)

_____

Use reading skills: Make judgments.

Good readers **make judgments** as they read. When you make a judgment, you bring what you know from your experience to help you understand the situation in the story. You might decide if a choice a character makes is the right one. You might also make a judgment about whether a character is a good person or not.

Make judgments.   In this story, Al has to make decisions about how to deal with a bad situation at work. Reread this section about one decision Al makes, and make a judgment about his actions.

> "Nice of you to join us," his boss Steve said sarcastically, even though Al was right on time. Al smiled briefly and went to his forklift. Then he shook his head. "What's that about?" Steve yelled. "You got a problem with me? With being on time?"
>
> Al paused to gather himself for a second. He stifled the urge he had to taunt Steve back. "I was on time, and you know it," Al said evenly, his voice tight. "Sorry if I seemed to be disrespectful." The rest of the day, both Steve and Al stayed clear of each other.

Al makes a decision about how to handle the conflict with his boss. What is your judgment of Al's actions? How did you reach that judgment?

_____

_____

_____

_____

Use a graphic organizer.

You can use a graphic organizer like the one below to help you make judgments. Fill in the organizer with the judgment you make about each of Al's actions below.

What you read	Your judgment about the action
Al tells Steve he'll try harder after he spills a pile of goods with his forklift.	1.
Al decides to talk to Steve about Steve's brother.	2.

Write About It

Write a summary.

Write a summary paragraph of the story you have just read. When you write a summary, you include the main points of a story. A summary of a story will include the most important characters and what happens to them. In a summary, you don't include unimportant details. In this case, you wouldn't include what Tami did at the beauty salon.

Prewriting   You can more easily write a summary of a story if you note the major events and the order in which they occurred. In the graphic organizer below, write these events on your own or with a partner. The first important event is written for you.

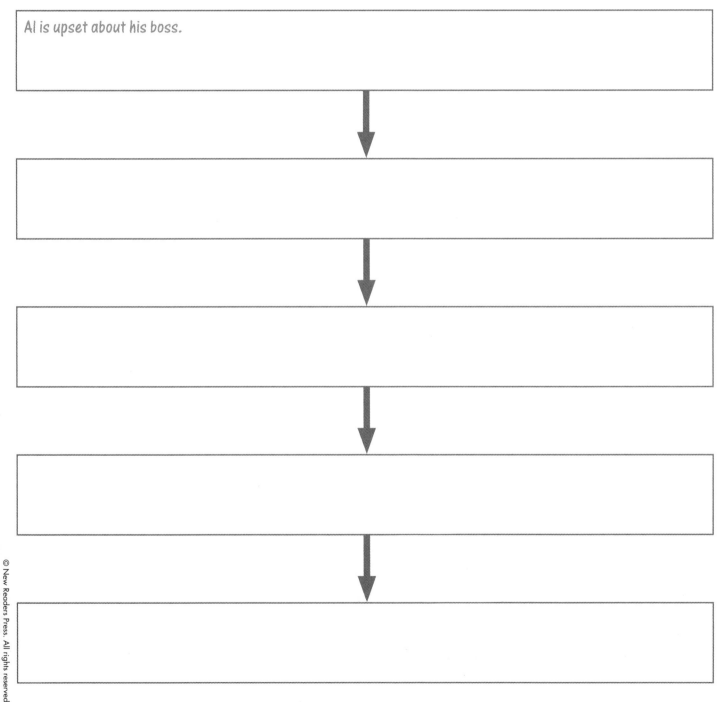

Al is upset about his boss.

Thinking Beyond Reading   Discuss the summary you plan to write with a partner. You can also explore the ideas further in the story by talking about these questions.

- Who are the characters in the story?

- What events are not important and should be left out?

- How does the story end?

Write a draft.   Write a first draft of your summary paragraph. Make sure you include the most important events in the story. Use the graphic organizer to help you. Write your summary so the events are in a clear order. You might begin your summary with this topic sentence: "Al is upset about his boss."

_____

_____

_____

_____

_____

_____

_____

_____

_____

_____

_____

_____

_____

_____

Revise and create a final draft.   Write your final draft on a separate piece of paper. As you revise, check your draft for these specific points:

- Did you write the most important events that happened?

- Did you write the summary so the events are in clear order?

- Did you check to make sure your spelling and grammar are correct?

The Changing Family

Learning Objectives

In this lesson you will:

▧ Read an article about the sandwich generation.

▧ Synthesize information.

▧ Master the key vocabulary used in the article.

▧ Write an explanation of how to help aging family members.

Key Vocabulary

circumstances *(noun)* conditions or events

increasingly *(adverb)* more and more

martyr *(noun)* a person who suffers in order to help others

nurtured *(verb)* helped someone or something develop

phenomenon *(noun)* a fact or event

population *(noun)* the number of people who live in a place

resentful *(adjective)* angry because you believe you have not been treated fairly

responsibilities *(noun)* duties

reversal *(noun)* a turn in the opposite direction

self-sufficient *(adjective)* able to take care of your own needs

Before You Read

Because they are involved in their reading, active readers find it easier to understand what they read. You can be an active reader by deciding what you want to learn (setting a purpose) and by asking yourself what the article has to do with your own life (making personal connections to the topic).

Set a purpose for reading.

1. What do you want to learn about the sandwich generation?

   _____

   _____

   _____

2. How might you use the information about the sandwich generation in your own life?

   _____

   _____

   _____

It's possible that I may have to take care of both my children and my parents someday. I'd like to find out what people in this situation can do.

Make personal connections to the topic.

1. Do you or does anyone you know have parents who are having difficulty living independently? Tell about that situation.

   _____

   _____

   _____

2. Do you know anyone who is taking care of their aging parents while raising their own children? Tell about that situation.

   _____

   _____

   _____

I have seen my cousin dealing with her ten-year-old son while she tries to handle her parents' medical problems. Sometimes she is worn out from all the demands on her time.

The Sandwich Generation

Do you picture yourself becoming part of the sandwich generation?
Underline or highlight sentences that define the sandwich generation.

Madge has to be at work in 15 minutes. Her son Sal is still in his pajamas. He is refusing to go to school. Her mother is standing in the doorway with her bathrobe on. She's asking Madge where the refrigerator is.

Welcome to the sandwich generation, Madge.

5 **Increasingly,** people in midlife are discovering that their duties aren't becoming fewer as they get older. Instead, the demands on their time, their energy, and their money are growing. These people are caught in a trap that sociologists call the sandwich generation. They are caught between the needs of their children and the needs of their aging parents. Some experts estimate

10 that there are about 16 million Americans in the middle of the "sandwich," with **responsibilities** for both the younger and older people in their families. That number is larger than the entire **population** of New England.

These numbers aren't going to get any smaller in the near future. In about 25 years, there will be more than 60 million Americans between the ages of

15 66 and 86 who may need help. In many cases, their children will be the ones to care for them.

The reasons for this growing **phenomenon** are easy to understand—people are living longer. A century ago, it was very unusual for someone to live to 90. But today it is far more common. Better health care and better living

20 conditions have led to much longer life spans. And as the population grows older, more and more people need help getting by.

midlife *(noun)*
middle age

sociologists *(noun)*
people who study how groups of people act

Another reason is that couples are having their children later in life. That means they have children at home at the age when their parents might have had all their kids out of the house.

1. What does the phrase "the sandwich generation" mean?

   _____

2. What are two causes of the sandwich generation?

   _____

   _____

In the next section, you will read how people feel when they suddenly find themselves caught between their parents and their children. Underline or highlight sentences that give information about what you can do to decide if people are able to take care of themselves.

25　　　Children who are taking care of their parents are often surprised by the change in **circumstances.** After all, their parents took care of them, **nurtured** them, and solved problems for them when they were children. This **reversal** of roles can be confusing and upsetting. One way to keep from feeling surprised at this shift in responsibility is to expect it. Although many older adults remain

30　**self-sufficient** for their entire lives, that is not always the case.

　　　The change in roles catches the elderly parents by surprise, too. Pride may cause them to lie about their ability to take care of themselves. Sometimes they simply don't understand that they need help. The best way to deal with this is to keep in touch. Don't take your parents' word that they're fine. Visit them

35　in their home. When you do, take a look in the refrigerator. See if it's filled with fresh, healthy food. See if the house is clean and neat. See if your parents' clothes are clean. Take a look at the mail. Are there piles of unpaid bills? Seniors who lose their ability to deal with finances often ignore their bills.

　　　If you decide that your parents need help with daily living, turn to other

40　close family members. Your brothers and sisters should be part of any decisions you make. They may also be able to help with the cost of taking care of your parents. If there are other family members who have close ties to your parents, they may want to help, too.

　　　There are other ways to get help for your parents. Call your state's general

45　help number. Ask for the phone numbers of agencies that deal with older people's problems. Every state has some support available for the elderly. And that help is often free.

3. How can you check to make sure your parents are able to take care of themselves at home?

_____

4. Who are the first people you should turn to if you think your parents need help with daily living?

_____

In the next section, you will read advice about how to help parents adapt to living with their children. Mark the paragraph that tells how to deal with children who still live at home when their grandparents come to stay.

Many people believe that the best way to take care of their parents is to have their parents move in with them. That can work, if people think about and discuss the decision. Experts advise people to begin by talking to their parents. Find out what your parents expect. And tell your parents what you expect in terms of financial help, time spent together, and so on.

Geriatric experts say it's an excellent idea to have a room ready for your parents. You can help make them feel at home by having them bring items from their own home.

Experts also suggest that you talk with your children so they know why life is changing. Discuss how the move will affect them. Outline their responsibilities to their grandparents, if they will have any. Be careful not to make your children feel **resentful** by giving them too many duties. Listen to your children. Make sure you address their concerns.

As you begin preparing for this major change, don't forget that the change may be hard on you, too. If your parents are able to help, it's likely that they will want to. Let them. You are not a superhero. Take time for yourself. It's not being selfish. Being squeezed inside the sandwich can be stressful, so don't be a **martyr.** If you're stressed out, you won't be much good to anyone.

Remember to take care of yourself. This way you can really enjoy the special experience of having three generations of your family living together in one place.

geriatric *(adjective)*
having to do with the problems of older people

5. What changes should you make in your home if your parents will be moving in?

_____

6. Why is it important for you to take time for yourself if your parents move in?

_____

After You Read

Build a robust vocabulary.

Writing Sentences   Write a complete sentence to respond to each of the following questions or statements. Use the underlined word in your answer. Use the definitions on page 25 to help you.

1. Describe a <u>self-sufficient</u> person.

   _____

2. Tell about a time when you felt <u>resentful</u>.

   _____

3. What is the <u>population</u> of your town?

   _____

4. Tell about some of your <u>responsibilities</u> at home.

   _____

5. Tell about someone who <u>nurtured</u> you when you were younger.

   _____

Sentence Completions   Complete each sentence using a word from the box.

circumstances	increasingly	martyr	nurtured	phenomenon
population	resentful	responsibilities	reversal	self-sufficient

1. In an unusual _____, the teacher sat down and asked the student to teach.

2. As he got more and more tired, he became _____ grumpy.

3. Under what _____ would you carry an umbrella?

4. A suicide bomber is someone who chooses to become a _____.

5. A strong earthquake is a _____ you don't want to be caught in.

Word Building   A **suffix** is a group of letters added to the end of a word. When a suffix is added, a new word with a new meaning is formed. The suffix *-ment* means the "act or result of." *Placement* is the act of placing. *Contentment* is the result of feeling content.

Read these words. Each ends with a suffix. Circle the suffix in each word.

| improvement | replacement | retirement | discouragement |

Use the meaning of the suffix to help you figure out what each word means. Write two sentences. Use one of the words above in each sentence.

1. _____

2. _____

TIP: When you come across a word you do not know, see if the word has a suffix or an ending you recognize, such as *-ment*, as in *employment*. If you know what the suffix means, you may be able to figure out the meaning of the word.

Writing Activity   Write a short paragraph that correctly uses key vocabulary words to describe the sandwich generation. Use at least four of the words from the list on page 25. Reread the definitions, if necessary.

_____

_____

_____

_____

_____

Think about your reading.

Check your comprehension.   Answer each question. If you don't know the answer, reread the lines in parentheses.

1. Why is the number of people in the sandwich generation growing? (lines 17–24)

_____

2. What can you do to decide if your parents need help with daily living? (lines 33–38)

_____

3. How can you get help from the state for older family members? (lines 44–47)

_____

4. If your parents are moving into your home, what should you explain to your children who are still living at home? (lines 56–60)

_____

Use reading skills: Synthesize information.

You **synthesize** when you take different pieces of information from what you read and weave them together to reach an understanding. For example, if you read about how to plant vegetable seeds, water them, weed the beds, and harvest the vegetables, you could synthesize that information and understand how to grow vegetables to eat.

Synthesize information.   In this article, you can synthesize information about who is in the sandwich generation. Read these sentences from the article.

> Increasingly, people in midlife are discovering that their duties aren't becoming fewer as they get older. Instead the demands on their time, their energy, and their money are growing. Some experts estimate that there are about 16 million Americans in the middle of the "sandwich," with responsibilities for both the younger and older people in their families.

Write a sentence that synthesizes the information above.

_____

Use a graphic organizer.

You can use a graphic organizer to help you synthesize information. Fill in the idea web below with information about getting ready to have your parents move in. In the outer ovals, write the details that tell what to do. You may need more or fewer ovals. Some are filled in for you.

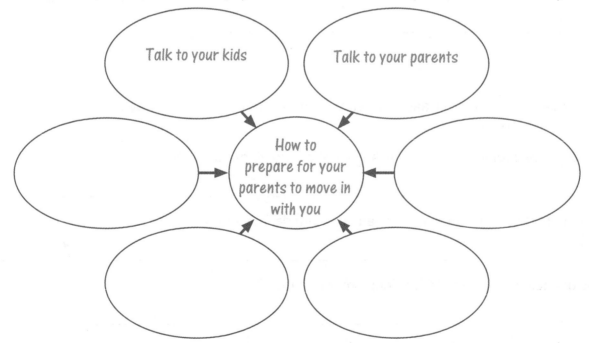

Write one or more sentences that synthesize the information in your graphic organizer.

Synthesis:

_____

_____

Write About It

Write an explanation.

Write a paragraph that explains how you or someone you know can help older family members. Think of the different ways you can make life easier for them. Use the graphic organizer below to organize your ideas.

Prewriting   Work on your own or with a partner. Fill in the graphic organizer to show your ideas. You will use the information in this graphic organizer to help you write.

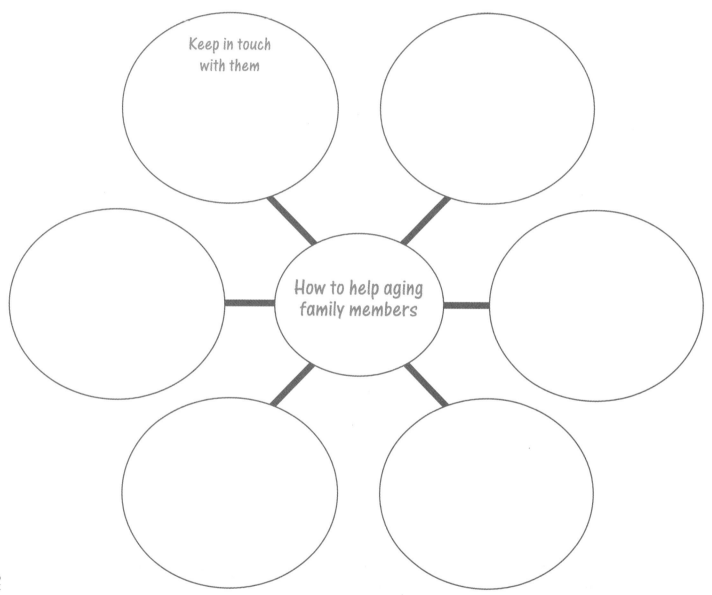

Thinking Beyond Reading   Think about these questions and discuss them with a partner. Add ideas to the graphic organizer as you talk.

- Do you think dealing with aging parents is a common problem? Why or why not?

- Why is it sometimes difficult to deal with aging parents?

- What can you do if you cannot get help from brothers and sisters?

Write a draft.   Write a first draft of your explanation. First tell what you plan to explain. You might begin like this: "As parents get older, they may need help with their daily lives. Here is how you can help them." Use the graphic organizer you completed to help you write your explanation.

_____

_____

_____

_____

_____

_____

_____

_____

_____

_____

_____

_____

_____

_____

_____

Revise and create a final draft.   Write your final draft on a separate piece of paper. As you revise, check your draft for these specific points:

- Did you write a topic sentence that sums up what the paragraph is about?

- Did you write a clear explanation of how you can help?

- Did you check the spelling and grammar to make sure your writing is clear and correct?

Keeping Neighborhoods Safe

Learning Objectives

In this lesson you will:

■ Learn about organizing a neighborhood crime watch program

■ Draw conclusions about what you read.

■ Master the key vocabulary used in the article.

■ Write a letter about a meeting to set up a neighborhood crime watch program.

Key Vocabulary

address *(verb)* to deal with

cohesive *(adjective)* sticking together tightly

efficiently *(adverb)* without waste

ensure *(verb)* to make certain

epidemic *(noun)* something that spreads very fast

expand *(verb)* to make larger

initiative *(noun)* the first step in making something happen

organizational *(adjective)* having to do with getting something started

persuade *(verb)* to get people to do or believe something

suspicious *(adjective)* not to be trusted

Before You Read

You know from the title that this article is about a community watch program. Begin your active reading by thinking of what you know about community watch programs. Then set a purpose for reading: decide what you want to learn from the article.

Use what you know.

1. What do you know about neighborhood crime watch programs?

_____

_____

_____

_____

Set a purpose for reading.

1. Why do you want to read this article?

_____

_____

_____

_____

2. What is one way you could use the information about neighborhood crime watch programs?

_____

_____

_____

_____

_____

Setting Up a Neighborhood Crime Watch

Neighborhood watch groups help people organize to reduce crime. Highlight or mark sentences in the article that tell you how they do it.

Feeling scared to walk down the street at night? Upset by graffiti everywhere? Tired of hearing stories of bikes stolen from garages and chairs stolen from front porches? Fight back. Begin a Neighborhood Watch program.

Neighborhood Watch groups are in communities large and small all
5 over the country. It's a simple idea. People in a neighborhood decide to become active in keeping their neighborhood safe. They organize and form a Neighborhood Watch.

In the United States, the National Sheriffs' Association (NSA) sponsors the nationwide program. Hundreds of communities are involved. All it
10 requires is someone to take the **initiative** and organize the neighborhood. Many resources are available through the NSA.

Neighborhoods often begin a watch program to deal with a specific problem. There may be an **epidemic** of burglaries. There may be a general increase in crime. Maybe the community is dealing with vandalism or graffiti.

15 If you have decided to organize a Neighborhood Watch, do your homework first. Go to your local police station and ask for materials on how to organize a program and information sheets on preventing crime. Also, the local law enforcement agency may be willing to come to talk at your **organizational** meeting.

20 Make flyers or write letters to neighbors and let them know about the meeting. The flyer should tell where and when the meeting is scheduled. It should tell what will be discussed at the meeting. It should tell what Neighborhood Watch is all about.

graffiti *(noun)*
  words or pictures illegally drawn on public spaces

association *(noun)*
  a group of people who have the same interest

vandalism *(noun)*
  needless damage or destruction of property

Before the meeting, you may want to visit people in your neighborhood to
25 **persuade** them to come to the meeting. Often, asking in person will **ensure** a
good turnout at the first meeting. Have the meeting after dinner, when more
people are likely to be available.

1. What group runs a nationwide Neighborhood Watch program?

   _____

2. How can you get people to come to the first meeting of a Neighborhood
   Watch group?

   _____

You're ready for the first meeting. Read on to find out what might happen.
Underline the sentences that tell what people do when they are part of
a Neighborhood Watch group.

Decide ahead of time what you want to discuss at the meeting so you use
everyone's time **efficiently.** At the meeting, explain the reason for the meeting
30 and have everyone introduce himself or herself. You will probably want to talk
about these topics:
- What is a Neighborhood Watch and how does it work?
- What concerns do you want to **address** about your neighborhood?
- What jobs will people have?
35 - How often, and where, should you meet?
Having a law enforcement officer at your meeting can attract people.
It also gives your meeting an official feeling. An officer can explain why
a Neighborhood Watch effort is important and stress that the police and
neighbors are partners in the effort. He or she can explain what other programs
40 have accomplished.
You will need to discuss the boundaries of the neighborhood. Some
neighborhoods are well defined. They have blocks and names that everyone
knows. Sometimes a very busy street or a boulevard helps to define a
neighborhood.
45 Neighbors need to know what they will do if they sign up for the
Neighborhood Watch. Explain that no one wants them to be vigilantes . They
will not be police officers with guns. They won't make arrests. They won't take
the place of police. Instead, explain that a Neighborhood Watch is just that—
a watch. Neighbors don't patrol. Instead, they keep an eye out for **suspicious**
50 behavior. They watch for things that are out of place.
One of the most important things people in a Neighborhood Watch group
do is to let one another know what is happening in the neighborhood. For
example, if there has been an increase in bike thefts, people in the group would
let one another know in order to prevent more thefts.

vigilantes *(noun)*
people who act illegally
to punish criminals

3. Why might you want to have a law enforcement officer at your first meeting?

_____

4. How could a Neighborhood Watch group be helpful if an increase in a certain kind of crime occurs?

_____

In the next section, you will read about some specific actions that Neighborhood Watch groups can take. Highlight or mark ideas that you think are most interesting.

55   There are many ways to **expand** the watch and help create a more **cohesive** community. Monthly meetings can be a chance for neighbors to get to know each other and to become more interested in watching out for each other. Neighbors who know each other notice when something doesn't
60   seem right. Neighbors can also set up networks to take in each other's mail during vacations and keep an eye on each other's houses when someone is away.

    Think about combining monthly watch meetings with other kinds of events that people enjoy. For example, a Fourth of July barbecue can get more
65   people involved. You can also plan programs on subjects that interest people, such as the best way to keep homes safe during vacations.

    Groups within your Neighborhood Watch might want to take on specific tasks. For example, one group might meet new neighbors and invite them to join. Another group might set up a "safe network" for the children. This means
70   that children are taught that a sign with a green hand in the window means that the house is a safe house with a friendly person who can help if they need it.

    Your Neighborhood Watch can be whatever you want it to be. Some are strictly business. They deal with crime and that's all. Other groups have
75   become much more. They have events such as neighborhood yard sales and fundraisers. Whatever shape your Neighborhood Watch takes, it can help the people in your neighborhood connect, it can keep crime down, and it can make the neighborhood feel more like a community.

5. What are some things that Neighborhood Watch groups do besides watching?

_____

6. What makes Neighborhood Watch groups work?

_____

After You Read

Build a robust vocabulary.

Writing Sentences   Write a complete sentence to respond to each of the following questions or statements. Use the underlined word in your answer. Use the definitions on page 35 to help you.

1. Can you <u>ensure</u> that people will join a Neighborhood Watch?

    _____

2. Give an example of <u>suspicious</u> behavior.

    _____

3. How could you <u>persuade</u> someone to join a Neighborhood Watch?

    _____

4. What is an <u>epidemic</u> of burglaries?

    _____

5. Tell about a way to <u>expand</u> a Neighborhood Watch.

    _____

Sentence Completions   Complete each sentence using a word from the box.

address	cohesive	efficiently	ensure	epidemic
expand	initiative	organizational	persuade	suspicious

1. Everyone knew it was time to _____ the problem of rising crime in the neighborhood.

2. Franco hated the _____ details of putting together the group.

3. Thom finished the job in ten minutes, and we told him he did it _____.

4. If we take the _____ to start a Neighborhood Watch group, we will all benefit.

5. We all think alike, which helps us be a _____ group.

Word Building   When you make the **past tense** of a verb, you usually add -*ed* to the present tense of the verb. For example, *pick* becomes *picked.* If there is an *e* on the end of the verb, you add only -*d*, as in *taste* and *tasted.*

But, sometimes you need to make spelling changes to make the past tense of a verb. If the last syllable of the word has a short vowel (for example, the *a* in *pat* or the *o* in *stop*), you double the consonant before adding -*d* or -*ed.* So *pat* becomes *patted and stop* becomes *stopped.*

Write the past tense for each of the verbs below. Then write a sentence using the past tense verb.

1. jump: _____

_____

2. mop: _____

_____

3. tame: _____

_____

4. fill: _____

_____

5. flip: _____

_____

TIP: Not every verb past tense is formed by adding -d or -ed. If there is no pattern, the verbs are called irregular verbs. You just have to know them. What is the past tense of *see?* It's *saw.* What is the past form of *eat?* It's *ate.* Reading and listening help you learn the past tense of irregular verbs.

Writing Activity Write a short paragraph that correctly uses key vocabulary words to explain why a Neighborhood Watch group might help your neighborhood. Use at least four of the words from the list on page 35. Reread the definitions, if necessary.

_____

_____

_____

Think about your reading.

Check your comprehension. Answer each question. If you don't know the answer, reread the lines in parentheses.

1. How can a local law enforcement agency help you set up a Neighborhood Watch group? (lines 16–19)

_____

2. What information should be included on a flyer for the first meeting? (lines 21–23)

_____

3. How does knowing your neighbors help keep crime down? (lines 58–61)

_____

4. How does a safe network for local kids work? (lines 68–71)

_____

Use reading skills: Draw conclusions.

When you **draw a conclusion,** you think about what you read. You add that to information you know from your life experiences. Then you put the information together to draw a conclusion. For example, you might know that a new school under construction is supposed to be completed in July. Then you read that there is a labor strike by construction workers. Based on what you know about construction and strikes, you can draw the conclusion that the school might not be completed on time.

Draw conclusions. In the first section of the article, you read how various communities form Neighborhood Watch programs to help reduce crime. You live in a community. You can draw the conclusion, based on what you read and what you know, that your neighborhood could also set up a Neighborhood Watch.

Reread this section of the article:

> Before the meeting, you may want to visit people in your neighborhood to persuade them to come to the meeting. Often, asking in person will ensure a good turnout at the first meeting. Have the meeting after dinner, when more people are likely to be available.

1. What did you learn about inviting people to the first meeting?

   _____

2. What do you know about your neighborhood?

   _____

3. What conclusion can you draw about the best way to ask people to attend a first meeting to form a Neighborhood Watch?

   _____

Use a graphic organizer.

Three sentences with information you read in the article are given below. Write what your experience tells you about each item. Then write a conclusion for each item.

What You Read	What You Know	Conclusion You Can Draw
1. People who want to start Neighborhood Watch programs often get information from local law enforcement agencies.		
2. Organizers tell neighbors they will not have to take the place of police officers.		
3. Neighborhood Watch meetings can include different things, from safety tips to barbecues.		

Write About It

Write a letter.

Write a letter you could use to invite your neighbors to a meeting to organize a Neighborhood Watch.

Prewriting   On your own or with a partner, create a graphic organizer like this web to help you decide what to write. Think of the purpose of the letter. What is the main thing you want to tell your neighbors? That is in the center oval. Then write the details that you also want them to know. Some suggestions are written for you. If you have more details you want to write, add another oval for each one.

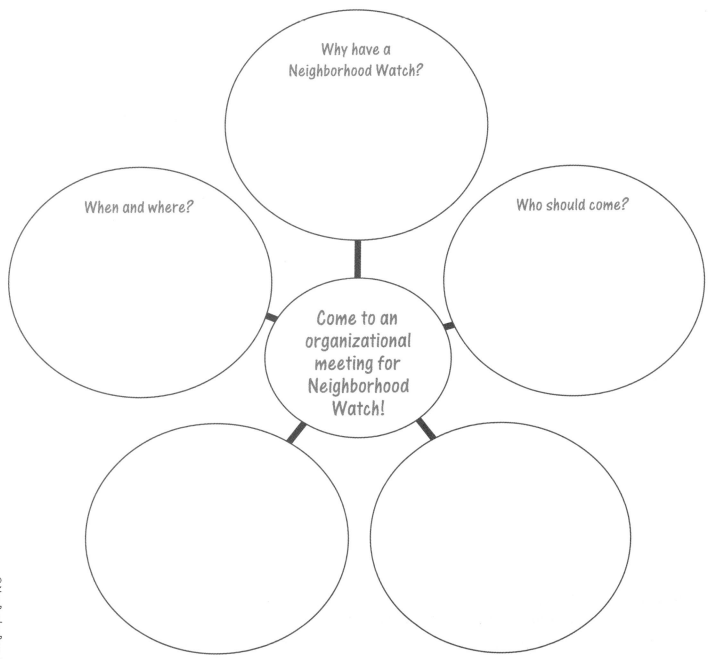

Thinking Beyond Reading   Think about these questions and discuss them with a partner. Add ideas to the graphic organizer as you talk.

- Do you think a Neighborhood Watch group can really do long-term good?

- Do you think your community would benefit from the group? Why?

- What would it take to be a good leader of a Neighborhood Watch group?

Write a draft.   On a separate piece of paper, write a first draft of your letter to the neighborhood. Follow the form of this letter, writing the heading, the body of the letter, and the closing as they appear here.

```
Your name
Your address


Date


Dear neighbor,


Body of letter













Sincerely,
Your signature
Your name
```

Revise and create a final draft.   Write your final draft on a separate piece of paper. As you revise, check your draft for these specific points:

- Did you include all the information someone would need to know about the meeting?

- Did you give good reasons for attending the meeting?

- Did you check to make sure your spelling and punctuation are correct?

Everyone Can Read

Learning Objectives

In this lesson you will:

▨ Read about a man who struggles to read.

▨ Compare and contrast.

▨ Master the key vocabulary used in the story.

▨ Write a paragraph to compare and contrast.

Key Vocabulary

abruptly *(adverb)* suddenly

descend *(verb)* to go down

despair *(noun)* the feeling of being without hope

enthusiasm *(noun)* a feeling of interest and excitement

floundering *(verb)* doing something in a clumsy way

foreboding *(noun)* the feeling that something bad is going to happen

impatiently *(adverb)* feeling annoyance

inspiration *(noun)* a really good idea

proficient *(adjective)* skilled and experienced

specifications *(noun)* detailed plans

Before You Read

As you begin reading this story, you know it will be about someone who can read, but can't read well. Begin by asking yourself an active reading question: What does saving a life have to do with reading well? Another good active reading strategy you might try is rereading something you don't fully understand.

Ask yourself questions.

THINK ABOUT IT

1. Why is the story called "To Save a Life?"

   _____

   _____

   _____

   _____

   _____

   _____

Stories often have titles that don't exactly tell what the story is about. How can learning to read save a life?

2. Why do some people have trouble learning to read?

   _____

   _____

   _____

   _____

   _____

   _____

Reread what you don't understand.

THINK ABOUT IT

When you read a difficult section of the article, reread it. Rereading will help you better understand what you read.

I'm not sure I understand what dyslexia is. I'll read the paragraph again, this time more slowly, and see if that helps me figure out the meaning.

To Save a Life

Cal has a secret he's desperate to keep and a situation he's desperate to change. Mark the sentences that tell Cal's secret.

Cal was terrified. He loved his job. He could solve any problem on the assembly line, fix it quickly, and get the line moving again. What he couldn't do well was read. And things were changing at work. He would soon be in charge of a new machine. His supervisor had tossed him
5 an instruction manual and said, "Here, Cal. Take a look. Here are all the **specifications** for the new line."

"Great," Cal said with as much **enthusiasm** as he could fake. "Yeah, great." As soon as the supervisor left, Cal threw the thick manual across the room.

Cal had heard they would be making changes, but he hadn't thought about
10 what that would mean for him. He hadn't thought that he might have to read a whole manual to run the new machine. He picked up the manual with **foreboding,** and looked through the chapters. The tiny print danced on the page. He couldn't read it. He couldn't even come close. What was he going to do? He put down the manual in **despair.** In a moment of self-pity, he got tears
15 in his eyes. Angrily, he blinked them away.

He had to figure out a solution. There had to be places that helped people like him who needed to read better. After **impatiently** looking in the phone book for about a half hour, Cal got the **inspiration** to call the local school district. Before he knew it, Cal was enrolled in a reading program for adult
20 learners. With a flicker of hope, he put down the phone. Maybe this time he wouldn't give up. Maybe this time he would learn to read well enough so that a new challenge at work was not a source of terror.

supervisor *(noun)*
> person in charge of other people at work

instruction manual *(noun)*
> a book that tells how something works or how to use it

1. Why does Cal throw the instruction manual at the beginning of the story?

_____

_____

2. Where does Cal find a reading program for adult learners?

_____

_____

Cal's tried to learn to read before. Why do you think he's had so much trouble? Make a prediction. Then find and underline the sentences that tell whether your prediction was right.

syllabus (noun)
a list of what a class will study

Despite his determination, Cal had to convince himself to put one foot ahead of the other and walk into the classroom. Classrooms were places of

25 failure. Inside the classroom were a dozen men and women of varying ages and colors. What they had in common, Cal thought, was the look of defeat. It was a look he shared with them.

The teacher, Mrs. Graves, handed out materials and went over the syllabus . Then she explained that at the end, they should all expect to be

30 more **proficient** readers. Cal sighed. He'd heard that before. He flipped through the pages. He felt a fog **descend** as the words danced before his eyes. He felt so stupid.

Cal struggled through the first lesson. He was already **floundering.** At the next class, Mrs. Graves listened to him read. Her eyes were fixed on him. At

35 the end of the class, she asked Cal to stay. They chatted as everyone picked up their books and left. She asked Cal about his job, what he liked about it, and what his duties were. She laughed as he described how he solved a problem with a simple solution that no one else had thought of. Then she opened a book and asked Cal to read. He struggled.

dyslexia (noun)
a physical condition in which people have difficulty reading

40 "That's enough," Mrs. Graves said **abruptly.** "Cal, has anyone ever told you that you might have dyslexia ?" He shook his head. "Dyslexia is a condition in which signals get crossed when you read. I think you have dyslexia. And I think I can help you."

3. Why does Mrs. Graves ask Cal to stay after class?

_____

_____

4. Why does Mrs. Graves think Cal is having so much trouble reading?

_____

_____

How might this time be different for Cal? What difference will that make for him? Mark the sentences that tell how Cal changes.

45   Mrs. Graves was as good as her promise. She brought in special reading materials for Cal. The materials focused on his reading problems. The process was frustrating. But Cal felt for the first time that he was really learning how to read. He didn't mind so much the hours he spent learning the skills Mrs. Graves was teaching. Unlike the other times he'd tried to learn to read, these lessons were sticking. He could see progress.

50   It took months, but by the end Cal was able to read more comfortably. He was no longer afraid of new reading materials. With Mrs. Graves' help, he'd made it through the manual for the new machine. At work, people noticed a difference in him.

    "Did you get married or something?" his supervisor asked. "You're sure

55 looking happy these days." Cal made a joke, but he realized that he was walking with swagger. He was more confident. He didn't hesitate to make suggestions. He had always been afraid that anything he suggested might mean he'd have to read something. Reading was still not a breeze. He continued to meet with Mrs. Graves, who was clearly happy with his progress.

60   She'd smile when he told her about another small victory at work. "She has every reason to be pleased with herself," Cal thought. "I should tell her."

    And so he did. "You saved my life," he told Mrs. Graves. "And that's not much of an exaggeration," he thought. "Not much at all."

5. Why does his supervisor ask Cal if he got married?

_____

_____

6. Why does Cal say Mrs. Graves saved his life?

_____

_____

After You Read

Build a robust vocabulary.

Writing Sentences   Write a complete sentence to respond to each of the following questions or statements. Use the underlined word in your answer. Use the definitions on page 45 to help you.

1.   If you <u>descend</u> a hill, are you at the top or the bottom when you finish?

_____

2.   What is something you are <u>proficient</u> at?

_____

3.   Tell what you have <u>enthusiasm</u> for.

_____

4.   When might you leave a place <u>abruptly</u>?

_____

5.   Explain why you need the right <u>specifications</u> if you are buying tires.

_____

Sentence Completions   Complete each sentence using a word from the box.

abruptly	descend	despair	enthusiasm	floundering
foreboding	impatiently	inspiration	proficient	specifications

1.   Cal put down the instruction manual in _____.

2.   "We have to go!" he said _____, tapping his foot.

3.   Cal got the _____ to call a school to ask about reading classes.

4.   The sheriff talked about the dangerous weather conditions with _____.

5.   When Cal tried to read, he found he was _____ because he could not make sense of the words.

Word Building   **Plurals** are words that mean *more than one*. You usually add -s or -es to make a word plural. But some plurals don't follow a pattern; they are irregular. There are two irregular plurals in this sentence from the story. Circle them.

Inside the classroom were a dozen men and women of varying ages and colors.

Compare your answers with a partner. Discuss what each word means.

Read the following words. Match each word with its plural form.

_____ 1. person   a. feet

_____ 2. foot   b. men

_____ 3. child   c. women

_____ 4. woman   d. children

_____ 5. man   e. people

Write three sentences. Use one of the plural words above in each sentence.

1. _____

2. _____

3. _____

TIP: When you read, you may find a word that you do not know. Use the context, or the words around the new word, to help you. Does the context describe more than one thing? If so, the new word might be an irregular plural.

Writing Activity Write a short paragraph that correctly uses key vocabulary words to imagine what it feels like to be unable to read well. Use at least four of the words from the list on page 45. Reread the definitions, if necessary.

_____

_____

_____

Think about your reading.

Check your comprehension. Answer each question. If you don't know the answer, reread the lines in parentheses.

1. What event caused Cal to look for a reading class to enroll in? (lines 3–6)

_____

2. When he walked in, what did Cal feel the people in the classroom had in common? (lines 26–27)

_____

3. How did learning to read better change Cal's attitude at work? (lines 54–58)

_____

4. Why did Cal think Mrs. Graves had every reason to be pleased with herself? (lines 60–63)

_____

Use reading skills: Compare and contrast.

When you **compare** things, you find how they are alike. When you **contrast** things, you tell how they are different. For example, you can compare an apple and an orange by saying they are both fruits. You can contrast them by saying that one is red and the other is orange.

Compare and contrast.   When you look at details in the story, you can compare and contrast Cal at the beginning and at the end.

1.   How is Cal the same at the beginning and at the end of the story?

_____

2.   How is he different at the beginning and at the end of the story?

_____

Use a graphic organizer.

You can use a Venn diagram like the one below to compare and contrast ideas. Fill in this Venn diagram to compare what you read at work and what you read at home.

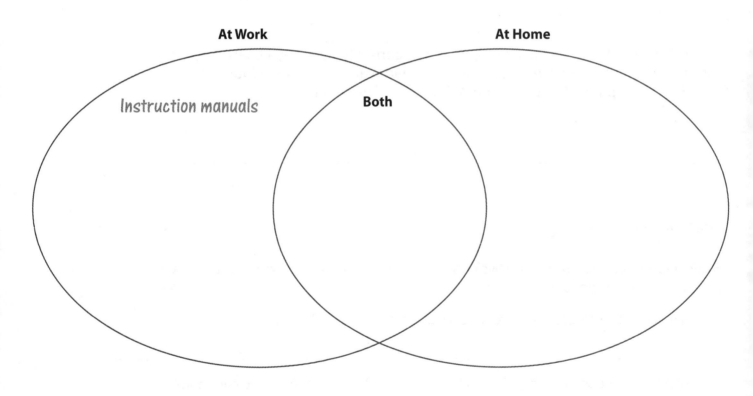

At Work   **At Home**

Instruction manuals   **Both**

Write About It

Write a paragraph to compare and contrast.

You can write a paragraph that tells how things are alike and different. Write a paragraph that tells how Cal changed and how he stayed the same before and after he took the reading class.

Prewriting   On your own or with a partner, write down ideas to include in your paragraph. Fill in the graphic organizer with your ideas about how things changed for Cal and how they stayed the same as he learned to read. You can include how he felt, how he acted, and what he did.

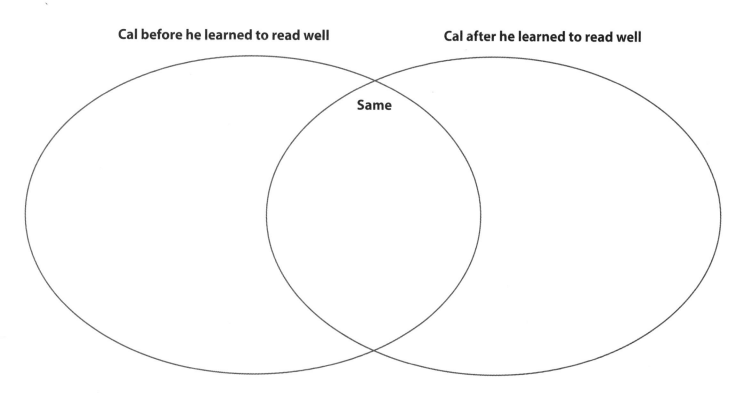

Cal before he learned to read well

Cal after he learned to read well

Same

Thinking Beyond Reading   Think about these questions and discuss them with a partner. Add ideas to the graphic organizer as you talk.

- Why do you think Cal didn't get help sooner?

- What kinds of problems did Cal face before he learned to read well?

- How do you think people acted differently towards Cal at the end?

Write a draft.   Write a first draft of your paragraph. Your paragraph might begin with this topic sentence: "Learning to read well changed Cal in some important ways, but in other ways, he was still the same person."

_____

_____

_____

_____

_____

_____

_____

_____

_____

_____

_____

_____

_____

_____

_____

_____

Revise and create a final draft.   Write your final draft on a separate piece of paper. As you revise, check your draft for these specific points:

- Did you show ways in which Cal changed after he learned to read well?

- Did you show ways in which Cal was the same after he learned to read well?

- Did you check spelling and grammar to make sure your writing is clear and correct?

A Crime-Fighting Agency

Learning Objectives

In this lesson you will:

▨ Learn about the Federal Bureau of Investigation.

▨ Identify main idea and details in what you read.

▨ Master the key vocabulary used in the article.

▨ Write a summary of the article.

Key Vocabulary

controversial *(adjective)* much argued about

enduring *(adjective)* lasting for a long time

infiltrated *(verb)* got inside of something without being noticed

intricate *(adjective)* complicated and full of details

preoccupation *(noun)* the condition of thinking about something so much that other things are forgotten

priorities *(noun)* things considered to be more important than other things

responsibility *(noun)* sense of duty; a job someone has to do

ruthless *(adjective)* cruel and without pity

technicians *(noun)* workers who have skill in a particular job

technology *(noun)* products developed using knowledge from science and industry

Before You Read

As you read the title and look at the picture, you will quickly figure out that this article is about the FBI. Before you begin to read, ask yourself these active reading questions: "What do I already know about the FBI? What would I like to learn about the FBI from reading this article?"

Use what you know.

1. What have you read or heard about the FBI?

   _____

   _____

   _____

   _____

   _____

2. Think of the information you have heard about the FBI. How accurate do you think that information is?

   _____

   _____

   _____

   _____

   _____

Set a purpose for reading.

1. What would you like to learn from this article?

   _____

   _____

   _____

   _____

   _____

"Open up. It's the FBI!"

From spies to gangsters, the FBI has seen it all. Highlight or mark each sentence that tells about the responsibilities of the FBI.

Coolly, the man draws his gun and shows his badge. "Freeze! I'm with the FBI!" The criminal is cornered. He thinks of running but instead throws up his hands.

Since its founding, the FBI, or Federal Bureau of Investigation, has caught
5 the attention of the American public. It takes on nationally known cases of kidnappings and murders. It also handles cases of **intricate** financial and computer crime. FBI agents catch people who spy against the United States. They also protect the United States against terrorists. In fact, that has become one of the FBI's top **priorities** in recent years.

10 The FBI was **controversial** when it was founded in 1908. Some people were worried about the national government having too much power. They felt that local police could take care of any crimes. Within a few years, though, most people came to agree that some crimes needed to be solved by a national agency. Among these crimes were those started in one state but continued in
15 another state, or those that had to do with the U.S. government.

Over the years, the FBI has focused on what the nation considers its greatest threats. In 1917, when World War I broke out, the FBI was put in charge of finding spies. In 1919, the FBI took **responsibility** for solving interstate crimes. Automobiles made trips across state lines easier and made it
20 harder for police officers to find the criminals.

interstate *(adjective)*
between states

1. Why was the FBI controversial in its early days?

_____

_____

2. Why did the FBI take charge of interstate crime?

_____

_____

The decades after the FBI was formed were filled with new crimes to focus on. Underline each new focus for the FBI.

The 1930s brought another era to the FBI. Back then, some Americans felt there was a national crime wave. Even today, many have heard of the criminals with names like "Baby Face" Nelson and "Machine Gun" Kelly. In truth, there was little evidence that the crime rate was worse. Even so, the FBI got

25 involved. That era led to one of the most **enduring** images of the FBI officer. He was seen as a tough fighter against **ruthless** gangsters. That image lives on today in movies that show FBI agents as fearless crusaders for justice.

The FBI's focus changed again in the 1940s when World War II began. The FBI was set to catch those who would spy on the United States. Sometimes,

30 those spies were from within the United States. In the 1950s, the Cold War between The Soviet Union and the United States became a national **preoccupation.** The FBI became responsible for catching Soviet spies. One big case was a joint American/English operation. It broke the Soviet Union's message code. The US and Britain used the decoded messages to identify spies.

35 In 1963, President John F. Kennedy was assassinated . At first, local police were in charge of the case. Then President Lyndon Johnson asked the FBI to take over. Now the FBI also investigates all murders of federal officials.

The 1960s marked the start of FBI interest in organized crime. These crime groups, known as "the mafia" or "the mob," ran operations that the FBI **infiltrated**

40 by using undercover officers. Beginning during that period, crime figures were prosecuted under new and powerful laws that aimed at organized crime.

assassinated (verb)
murdered

prosecuted (verb)
put on trial in a court of law

3. How did breaking the Soviet Union's code help the United States during the Cold War?

_____

_____

4. What two types of crime did the FBI concentrate on in the 1960s?

_____

_____

Read on to find what changes have taken place at the FBI. Underline each change that you read about.

There have been changes in priorities at the FBI in recent years. The serious concern with terrorism began with the first bombing of the World Trade Center in 1993. Terrorism has been one of the priorities of the FBI ever
45 since. That focus has grown stronger since the attacks of September 11, 2001.

The FBI also is involved with the fairly new category of Internet and computer crime. These nationwide crimes are often committed using programs that damage computers. They can also be thefts of money and identity. In these cases, criminals break into computer files to get information. The FBI has
50 been successful in solving many of these cases.

The FBI has long been a leader in using **technology** to solve crimes. The focus on tools to solve crimes began early. In 1924 the agency put together a system for identifying fingerprints. In recent years, the FBI has taken a role in developing accurate DNA testing. In this kind of testing, **technicians** can
55 match material such as hair or skin with the person it came from. Local and state police officers with difficult cases often use the FBI lab.

Because of the growing scope of the FBI's work, the agency needs to hire a wider variety of people than it once did. For years, only men were FBI agents. That rule has changed. Now the FBI hires women as well. Once, people who
60 applied for jobs had to have college degrees in law or accounting. Now, the FBI is also looking for people who speak other languages and who are skilled computer technicians. Every special agent for the FBI must have a college degree. Agents must also be physically fit. They must pass a drug test. They must be between the ages of 23 and 37. The process of hiring takes a long time.
65 Those who are hired must agree to spend three years as FBI agents. Despite all this, becoming an FBI agent is very competitive. Saying, "It's the FBI. Open up," hasn't lost its glamour.

5. What breakthrough happened in the FBI crime lab in 1924?

_____

_____

6. How can identifying DNA help to solve crimes?

_____

_____

After You Read

Build a robust vocabulary.

Writing Sentences   Write a complete sentence to respond to each of the following questions or statements. Use the underlined word in your answer. Use the definitions on page 55 to help you.

1. What is something that could be <u>controversial</u>?

    _____

2. What is something <u>technicians</u> in a crime lab might do?

    _____

3. What are some <u>priorities</u> you have for today?

    _____

4. Who has the <u>responsibility</u> for cooking in your family?

    _____

5. Name something that could have an <u>intricate</u> design.

    _____

Sentence Completions   Complete each sentence using a word from the box.

controversial	enduring	infiltrated	intricate	preoccupation
priorities	responsibility	ruthless	technicians	technology

1. The agent's _____ with the crime was so strong that he worked most evenings.

2. DNA matching is an example of a _____ that the FBI helped to develop.

3. The _____ image of an FBI agent is that of a brave crime fighter with a gun.

4. The agent _____ the group in order to find out if spies were within the United States.

5. They are considered _____ criminals.

Word Building   Look at the following words. What is the same about all of them?

fireplace	kickoff	heartfelt	downgrade	jailbreak

Each word is a **compound word.** It is made up of two smaller words.

Discuss what each word means. Use the meanings of the smaller words to help you define each compound word.

Read these compound words. Draw a line between the two parts of each word. Tell what each word means.

| highway | bulletproof | paperback | lawmaker | courthouse |

Write two sentences. Use one of the compound words above in each sentence.

1. _____

2. _____

TIP: When you see long words you do not recognize, try to divide them into two words. If you find two words, look closely to decide if the meanings of the two words can help you understand the compound word's meaning.

Writing Activity   Write a short paragraph that correctly uses key vocabulary words to tell about the work of the FBI. Use at least four of the words from the list on page 55. Reread the definitions, if necessary.

_____

_____

_____

_____

_____

Think about your reading.

Check your comprehension.   Answer each question. If you don't know the answer, reread the lines in parentheses.

1. Why was the FBI controversial at first? (lines 10–12)

_____

2. What was the FBI's main interest in the 1940s? (lines 28–30)

_____

3. What kinds of computer crimes does the FBI get involved with now? (lines 46–50)

_____

4. What are two kinds of work done in the FBI's crime lab? (lines 52–56)

_____

Use reading skills: Identify main idea and details.

The **main idea** is the most important point of a paragraph or even a whole article. The **details** are facts or any other information that supports the main idea.

Identify main idea and details. Reread this section from the article. As you read, decide what the main idea of the section is.

> Every special agent for the FBI must have a college degree. Agents must also be physically fit. They must pass a drug test. They must be between the ages of 23 and 37. The process of hiring takes a long time. Those who are hired must agree to spend three years as FBI agents. Despite all this, becoming an FBI agent is very competitive.

1. What is the main idea of the section?

   _____

2. What are some details that support that main idea?

   _____

Use a graphic organizer.

You can use a graphic organizer like this idea web to help you organize main ideas and details. A main idea is written in the center oval. Complete this web by writing details that support this main idea in the smaller ovals. One of the details is already written for you.

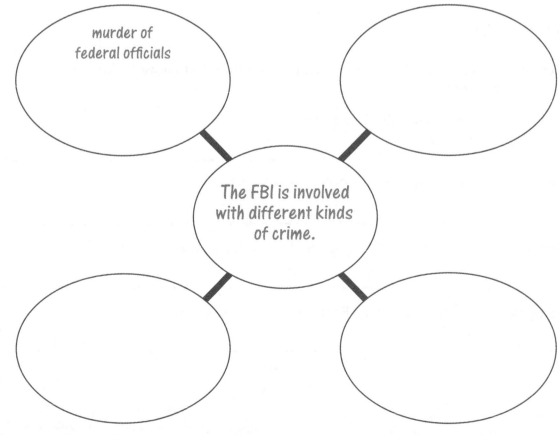

murder of federal officials

The FBI is involved with different kinds of crime.

Write About It

Write a summary.

Write a summary of the article "Open up. It's the FBI!" Your summary should tell the main idea of the article and then list the details that support this main idea. This is different from writing a summary of a story where you tell the important events in the order they happened.

Prewriting   Use this graphic organizer to help you decide on the main idea and the important details you want to include in the summary you will write. To complete the graphic organizer, first review the article and decide what the main idea of your summary will be. Write the main idea in the center oval. Then list supporting details in the other ovals.

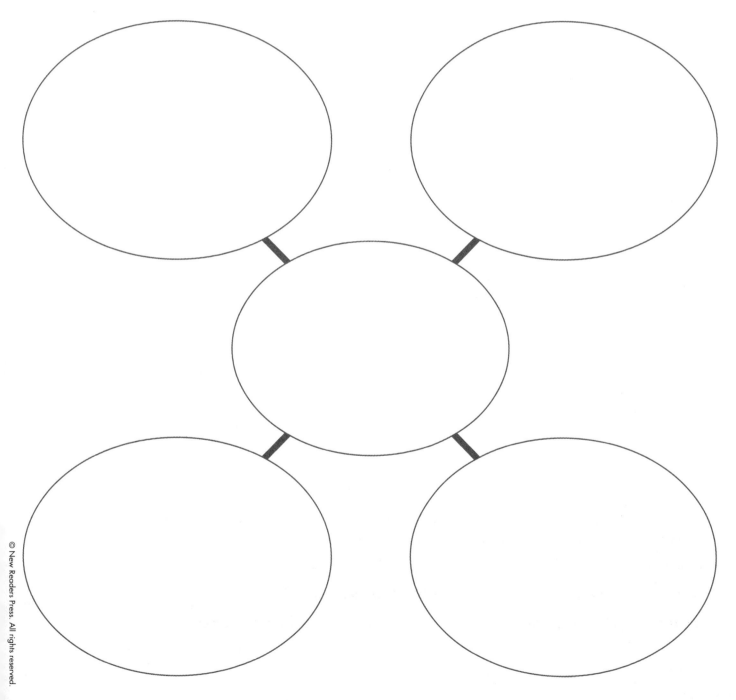

Thinking Beyond Reading   Think about these questions and discuss them with a partner. Add ideas to the graphic organizer as you talk.

- What opinion do most Americans have of the FBI today?

- Why do you think the FBI has been in the news so much in recent years?

- Why do you think so many people still want to be FBI agents?

Write a draft.   Write a first draft of your summary. Remember that a summary is short, and tells only the main points and the most important details that support those main points. Your summary might begin with this topic sentence: "The FBI has gone through many changes since its founding and has become a very important national agency."

_____

_____

_____

_____

_____

_____

_____

_____

_____

_____

_____

_____

_____

_____

_____

Revise and create a final draft.   Write your final draft on a separate piece of paper. As you revise, check your draft for these specific points:

- Does your summary tell the main point of the article you read?

- Does your summary list the details that support that main points?

- Did you check to make sure your spelling, grammar, and punctuation are correct?

Opportunities Lost and Found

Learning Objectives

In this lesson you will:

▓ Read a story about a streetball tournament.

▓ Make inferences.

▓ Master the key vocabulary used in the story.

▓ Write a paragraph about sports.

Key Vocabulary

annoyance *(noun)* an irritation

deflated *(adverb)* feeling let down

desperation *(noun)* a strong feeling that you will do anything to change a bad situation

disheveled *(adjective)* messy

explosively *(adverb)* with a burst of energy

humility *(noun)* the quality of not being too proud of yourself

incubator *(noun)* a place for developing or growing things

phenomenon *(noun)* a person with an unusual ability who attracts attention

pirouette *(noun)* the act of whirling or turning the body on the toe of one foot

startled *(adjective)* slightly shocked or surprised

Before You Read

Try using these active reading strategies to get the most out of what you read. Ask yourself questions as you read or visualize what you read. Both strategies can be especially helpful in getting the most out of fiction.

Ask yourself questions.

1. What is streetball?

   _____

   _____

   _____

   _____

   _____

Visualize while you are reading.

1. Read the first paragraph. Picture in your mind T.J. sitting on the stoop, bouncing the basketball. Describe the setting.

   _____

   _____

   _____

   _____

   _____

Slam Dunk

It may be the last chance for Friz to have the life he dreams of. Underline the sentence that tells how Friz lost his opportunity to play college basketball.

T.J. sat idly on the stoop, bouncing the basketball from hand to hand. He peered down the street, looking for Dwayne and Eddy. Then he saw them. "C'mon, Friz," he yelled to his brother, still inside. Friz came outside. He was his usual **disheveled** self. His wild hair was in a halo around his head, his shoes
5 were untied.

They walked to the court, the ball bouncing among them. "Did you guys hear about the streetball tournament?" asked Dwayne. "I heard the winning team will go to a national championship. They say there'll be scouts there from the NBA."

10 "Right," muttered Friz, his head down. He bounced the ball from hand to hand. Only T.J. knew how much Friz wanted Dwayne to be right. Friz had had a brilliant career in basketball all during high school. But he'd been arrested for a DUI right after graduation, and lost his college scholarship. The college rep had said it was because of "regulations." That had been the end of that. But
15 Friz was good. Really good. One of the best players in the city. They once said he was a shoe-in for the NBA. Now at the age of 20, he was a has-been.

"No, really," Dwayne said. He brought out a crumpled sheet of paper. "Look." Friz and T.J. read the paper. It did look real. Recently NBA scouts had been paying attention to the streetball games. They realized that streetball was
20 a huge **incubator** for basketball talent. For the first time in months, T.J. saw something in Friz's eyes. It looked like hope.

streetball (noun)
   a type of basketball game played mainly in cities

scouts (noun)
   people who look for talented players for professional teams

1. How do you think Friz may have gotten his nickname?

_____

_____

2. Why did Friz lose his scholarship to college?

_____

_____

Friz has a bit of hope that he can still make it in basketball. Do you think he'll try to play in the tournament? When you find the answer, underline it.

    So Friz started to play with the Rockets, the best team in the area. They looked unstoppable. Everyone on the team had the same hopes as Friz. But they all knew that Friz was king of the court. Just watching him play was a
25   joy. Friz could spin and float to the rim, slam in the ball, and **pirouette** to the ground.

    Friz and the rest of the team played whenever they could get off work. T.J. also began going to the courts. It was fun to watch the Rockets play. Once while he was there, another team showed up. They were called the Monarchs.
30   They were all friends, but guys on both teams were hoping to win and go to the tournament. They got into a game. The Monarchs were one man short, so they asked T.J. to join them.

    The Rockets had a bit of an attitude. They expected to win. The Monarchs were giving them trouble, though. Everyone played hard every second of
35   the game, and it showed. The Monarchs won. Friz and his team were left losers. They stood **deflated** at the edge of the court. They had played like the Monarchs were a mere **annoyance,** nothing to worry about. Big mistake. It turned out to be a good thing, however. "A little **humility** never hurt any team," T.J. thought.
40   The Monarchs asked T.J. to join them permanently. He agreed. The Rockets had never asked him.

3. Why did T.J. join the Monarchs?

_____

_____

4. Who won when the Rockets and Monarchs played?

_____

_____

Friz feels that winning this tournament might be his last chance for the NBA. Continue reading to find out what happens. Put an arrow in the margin where you find out.

The tournament got underway. There were more players and more people in the stands than T.J. had expected. Nobody was too surprised when the Rockets made the finals. And no one was too surprised when the Monarchs
45 made the finals as well. That game would decide who went on to the championship tournament with the NBA scouts.

T.J. found himself getting excited. Friz was such a basketball **phenomenon** that T.J. got little attention. He had been a star himself in school. He was nothing like Friz, but very few players were. T.J. was a fine player, though, and he
50 liked his teammates. He felt proud that he was in the final game just like Friz.

The game started **explosively.** Friz quickly scored a series of field goals that put the Rockets up 10 to 4. Friz was really working it. T.J. knew that Friz saw this as his last chance to make the NBA. He had told T.J. how much he wanted to get to the championship tournament.

55 At first the Monarchs were **startled** by the way Friz was playing. They backed off. Soon they got it together and tied the game. Friz's eyes were dark and wide as he pumped in point after point. But T.J. knew that Friz was playing with some **desperation.** Friz really did see this as a do-or-die game. He'd told T.J. so. His longing for a different basketball life was fierce in his eyes. It almost
60 scared T.J.

The two teams kept up with each other, basket for basket. Friz was clearly driving the Rockets. But the Monarchs had several players who were also having huge successes. T.J. wasn't doing badly either. He was hitting his shots better than he could remember.

65 As the minutes ticked down, Friz got more frantic. He raced down the court and went after each rebound. The sweat was flying from the crazy hair that gave him his nickname.

In the last seconds of the game, the Monarchs were two points down. The final shot came to T.J. He froze. "If I make the basket, Friz loses his dream. If I
70 miss, Friz gets a chance." T.J. paused. He threw the ball, a lovely arc right toward the basket. The ball hit the rim and bounced off. The Rockets won 87 to 85.

"Did I miss the basket on purpose?" T.J. wondered. He rubbed his chin and thought to himself, "I don't think I'll ever know for sure."

field goals (noun)
in basketball, shots through the hoop, good for two points

5. Why was Friz so intent on making it to the championship game?

_____

_____

6. Why do you think T.J. froze before he took the last shot?

_____

_____

After You Read

Build a robust vocabulary.

Writing Sentences   Write a complete sentence to respond to each of the following questions or statements. Use the underlined word in your answer. Use the definitions on page 65 to help you.

1. Name an <u>annoyance</u> in your life.

    _____

2. Tell about a time when you felt <u>startled</u>.

    _____

3. When do you look <u>disheveled</u>?

    _____

4. If you speak <u>explosively</u>, how are you speaking?

    _____

5. Name a sports figure you think is a <u>phenomenon</u>.

    _____

Sentence Completions   Complete each sentence using a word from the box.

annoyance	deflated	desperation	disheveled	explosively
humility	incubator	phenomenon	pirouette	startled

1. As he leaped with the ball in the air, he did a _____.

2. Streetball is sometimes considered an _____ for pro basketball.

3. Friz realizes with _____ that this may be his last chance for an NBA future.

4. The proud team felt real _____ when they lost the game.

5. When he didn't make the shot, he felt let down and _____.

Word Building   **Prefixes** are groups of letters that go before a word to change the word's meaning. For example, the prefix *re-* means "to do again." The word *repaint* means "to paint again." Look at the common prefixes in the chart below.

Prefix	Meaning
mis-	wrong, bad
over-	too, too much
pre-	before
un-	not

Look at the words below. Underline the prefix in each. Check your answers with a partner. What does each word mean?

unbelievable	**misspell**	**prepay**	**overpay**

Add the prefix *mis-, over-, pre-,* or *un-* to each word in the sentences below. Use the context, or the words around the word, to tell which prefix to add.

1. The meat was _____ cooked because we left it in the oven too long.

2. The words on the computer screen were _____ clear and hard to read.

3. If you _____ set the temperature in the oven, it will be hot when you need it.

4. Marta _____ understood the question and answered incorrectly.

5. Earl _____ ate and felt sick.

TIP: You may be able to use what you know about prefixes to tell what an unknown word means. For example, knowing the prefix *bi-* (two) will help you understand that *bimonthly* means "twice a month."

Writing Activity   Write a short paragraph that correctly uses key vocabulary words to tell about the game as if you were watching Friz play. Use at least four of the words from the list on page 65. Reread the definitions, if necessary.

_____

_____

_____

Think about your reading.

Check your comprehension.   Answer each question. If you don't know the answer, reread the lines in parentheses.

1. Why is Friz a has-been in basketball? (lines 11–16)

_____

2. Why didn't T.J. play for the Rockets? (lines 40–41)

_____

3. Why did Friz play so hard in the tournament game against the Monarchs? (lines 52–54)

_____

4. What role did T.J. play at the end of the story? (lines 68–73)

_____

Use reading skills: Make inferences.

When you **make inferences,** you add what is in the reading to what you already know. For example, if you read, "As Janice stepped outside, she shivered," you make an inference that it is cold. People shiver when they are cold.

Make inferences.   Read these sentences from the story. Write inferences you can make.

> They realized that streetball was a huge incubator for basketball talent. For the first time in months, T.J. saw something in Friz's eyes. It looked like hope.

1. Inference: _____

> Nobody was too surprised when the Rockets made the finals. And no one was too surprised when the Monarchs made the finals as well. That game would decide who went on to the championship tournament with the NBA scouts.

2. Inference: _____

> T.J. had been a star himself in school. He was nothing like Friz, but very few players were. T.J. was a fine player, though, and he liked his teammates. He felt proud that he was in the final game just like Friz.

3. Inference: _____

Use a graphic organizer.

You can use a graphic organizer to help you make inferences. Fill in the diagram below to make an inference about the story.

What You Read	What You Know
T.J. paused. He threw the ball, a lovely arc right toward the basket. The ball hit the rim and bounced off. The Rockets won 87 to 85. "Did I miss the basket on purpose?" T.J. wondered. He rubbed his chin and thought to himself, "I don't think I'll ever know for sure."	

Inference You Make

Write About It

Write a paragraph about the game.

Write a paragraph summing up the tournament game between the Monarchs and the Rockets. Tell what happened, making sure you let the reader know the final score.

Prewriting   You can use the flowchart below to help you decide what to write in your paragraph. Start off by telling the final score. The rest of your paragraph should give details about the game in the order in which they happened.

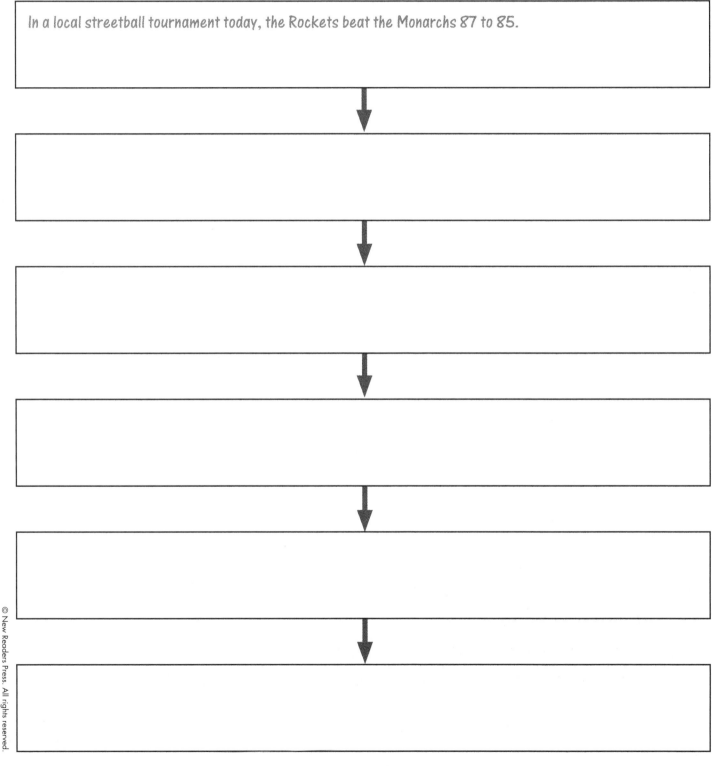

In a local streetball tournament today, the Rockets beat the Monarchs 87 to 85.

Thinking Beyond Reading   Think about these questions and discuss them with a partner. Add ideas to the flowchart as you talk.

- How would you describe the relationship between T.J. and Friz?

- What do you know about Friz's personality? Can he succeed in the NBA?

- What would you have done if you had been T.J.?

Write a draft.   Write a first draft of your story. Your paragraph might begin with a topic sentence like this: "Today the Monarchs and Rockets played at the Hill Street basketball court to see which team will go to the championship."

_____

_____

_____

_____

_____

_____

_____

_____

_____

_____

_____

_____

_____

_____

Revise and create a final draft.   Write your final draft on a separate piece of paper. As you revise, check your draft for these specific points:

- Did you explain why the game was important?

- Did you tell readers the final score?

- Did you tell what happened in the order in which it happened?

- Did you check spelling and grammar to make sure your writing is clear and correct?

Traveling on Two Wheels

Learning Objectives

In this lesson you will:

▨ Learn about motor scooters.

▨ Classify information that you read.

▨ Master the key vocabulary used in the article.

▨ Write a how-to paragraph about how to buy a motor scooter.

Key Vocabulary

alternative *(noun)* one of two or more choices

complexity *(noun)* the condition of having a large number of parts

consideration *(noun)* a reason for doing something

convertible *(noun)* a car with a roof that can be removed or folded back

environmental *(adjective)* referring to the earth, air, and water surrounding people, plants, and animals

impact *(noun)* a strong, powerful effect

inferior *(adjective)* of poorer quality than something else

maneuver *(verb)* to move in a skillful way

mechanical *(adjective)* having to do with machines or motors

residential *(adjective)* having to do with places where people live

Before You Read

You may not know exactly what a scooter is, but you can tell from the illustration and the title that this article is about motor scooters. Think of scooters you have seen and what you know about them as you begin to read. Also set a purpose for reading. Ask yourself: "What do I want to learn from reading this article?"

Use what you know.

THINK ABOUT IT

1. Cars, buses, and trains are the most common ways people get around. How do you get to work or school?

   _____

   _____

   _____

When I drive my car to work, I often sit in traffic for half an hour or more. This is a waste of my time and money. I wonder if there's a better way for me to get to work.

2. What do you like about the way you get around?

   _____

   _____

   _____

3. What don't you like about the way you get around?

   _____

   _____

   _____

Set a purpose for reading.

THINK ABOUT IT

1. How could you use information about scooters?

   _____

   _____

   _____

With gas costing so much, perhaps a scooter would be a good way to get around town. I'll read to find out if getting a scooter makes sense.

Scooter Story

Are you tired of the high costs of driving a car? Maybe it's time to cut back to two wheels. Highlight or mark sentences that tell why you may want to replace your car with another way to get around.

The price of gas is reaching record levels. People are concerned about the **environmental** effect of burning gas. So, to many people, motor scooters are looking like a good **alternative** to driving cars.

Scooters, Mopeds, and Motorcycles

5   From mopeds to motorcycles, there are a variety of different kinds of two-wheeled motor vehicles legally driven on streets. Some are mopeds, or motorized bicycles. They look like bicycles, and they cannot go fast. The fastest mopeds go about 30 miles an hour.

Scooters are a step up from mopeds in speed and **complexity.** Scooters can
10   go faster—some can even go 80 miles an hour, although most do not go more than 40 or 50 miles an hour. Scooters are usually heavier than mopeds and have larger engines. Most scooters have smaller wheels than either mopeds or motorcycles. Legally, because some scooters can travel at local speed limits, scooters are usually considered motorcycles, and you need a motorcycle license
15   to drive one.

Scooters and motorcycles look very different. On a motorcycle, you ride on the engine and get on the motorcycle by swinging your leg over the high seat. The gas tank is usually between your knees. On a scooter, you step on as if you were getting ready to sit in a chair. The engine is usually in the back of the
20   scooter. The gas tank may be in the floorboard or in the back of the scooter.

vehicles *(noun)*
  things used to carry and move people or things from one place to another

motorized *(adjective)*
  powered by a motor

Most motorcycles go much faster than scooters, even as fast as 100 miles an hour. Motorcycles are also much heavier than scooters, and their wheels are much larger than scooter wheels. Your feet rest on the floorboard of a scooter. On a motorcycle, your feet rest on foot pegs.

1. Why are people interested in motor scooters today?

   _____

2. Do you think that a scooter sounds good?

   _____

Read on to find out if one is right for you. Underline reasons scooters would work for you, and circle reasons scooters would not work for you.

commute *(noun)*
a daily trip from home to work and back

Should You Buy a Scooter?

25   Is a motor scooter right for you? Here are some things to consider. First, think about what you need transportation for. If you just need to zip around town, or have a short commute to work, a scooter might be just the thing. If you want transportation for getting around town that costs less to buy and

30   less money to run, a scooter may be a good choice. Scooters cost less than cars and get 60 to 100 miles a gallon, which means you spend less on gas than for cars that often get 20 miles a gallon or less.

For some people, buying a scooter is attractive because of its lower cost, but another key reason to buy one is its smaller environmental **impact.**

35   Scooters use much less gas, which means less oil taken from the ground and less pollution pumped into the air.

Scooters don't work for everyone, though. If you live in a very rainy or snowy place, you might often find yourself uncomfortable riding a scooter. There's no protection from the weather on a scooter. Unlike a **convertible,**

40   you can't put up the top.

Also, think about your commute. If you travel a long distance to work, much of it on highways, you may want the speed and protection a car offers. On the other hand, if you have a short commute and parking is an issue, a scooter may be an excellent choice since it is easy to **maneuver** and easy to park.

45   ### Scooter Rules

If you buy a scooter, you should think about safety and rules, too. You will likely need a motorcycle license to operate your scooter. In most states, that means reading a state manual , taking a written test, and also taking a driving test. To stay safe, buy a helmet, gloves, and good boots. When you are on a

50   scooter, you are less protected. It pays to buy good equipment to keep safe.

manual *(noun)*
a book of rules or instructions

3. List two reasons to think about getting a scooter for a commute.

_____

4. Why is a scooter not always a good choice for someone who lives a long distance from work?

_____

You've decided to buy a two-wheeled motor vehicle. Read on to find out how to choose one. Put a star in the margins where you read good advice.

Choosing a Scooter

You've made the decision to buy a scooter. Now, how do you pick one as you look at all the choices? First, begin by thinking about the differences among scooters, motorcycles, and mopeds. Which one you buy depends on
55 how much you have to spend and how you plan to use the vehicle.

If you decide to buy a scooter, you still have more thinking to do. Scooters are less expensive than cars, but their costs can vary widely. Think about buying a used scooter if money is a **consideration.** If you buy a new scooter, you may find that you will pay more for the better-known brand. Many think the
60 extra cost is worth it to get a well-known and reliable brand of scooter, though.

You also need to think about how comfortable you feel with **mechanical** things. In some scooters, when you fill the gas tank, you pour motor oil into one place in the scooter and put gas in the other. Some people feel that having to do this is too much trouble.

65 You may also want to choose your scooter based on how you will use it. If you are mainly using it to get around town on **residential** streets, a low-power scooter may be the best idea. If you plan to use the scooter on highways, you will need the extra speed of a larger engine.

Make sure the scooter you choose comes from a respected company, and
70 that it is covered by a warranty . You will want to know a good place to get service. Scooters bought online may be cheaper, but some people have gotten **inferior** scooters this way.

If you choose your scooter carefully, you will have made a wise investment. It will pay you back with good gas mileage, and its smaller size makes it easier
75 to park. Overall, it is an economical decision.

warranty (noun)
a written promise to fix or replace something

5. Why is it sometimes better to buy a used scooter?

_____

6. List three things you should consider when buying a scooter.

_____

After You Read

Build a robust vocabulary.

Writing Sentences Write a complete sentence to respond to each of the following questions or statements. Use the underlined word in your answer. Use the definitions on page 75 to help you.

1. What is a <u>convertible</u>?

_____

2. Name an <u>environmental</u> problem.

_____

3. What is a <u>residential</u> area?

_____

4. Do you like <u>mechanical</u> things?

_____

5. Why might an <u>inferior</u> bike cost less?

_____

Sentence Completions Complete each sentence using a word from the box.

alternative	complexity	consideration	convertible	environmental
impact	inferior	maneuver	mechanical	residential

1. Burning fossil fuels has a big _____ on pollution.

2. Driving a motor scooter is an _____ to driving a car.

3. Some people buy a cheaper form of transportation when money is a _____.

4. Cars have more _____ because they have more complicated parts than motor scooters do.

5. A small scooter is easier to _____ in tight places than a car.

Word Building A **suffix** is a group of letters added to the end of a word. When a suffix is added, a new word with a new meaning is formed. The suffix *-or* or *-er* can describe what someone does. An *actor* is someone who acts. The suffix *-less* means "without." The word *harmless* means "without harm."

Write the meaning of each word. Use the meanings of the suffixes to help you figure out what the words mean. Then use each word in a sentence.

1. player: _____

   _____

2. homeless: _____

   _____

3. collector: _____

   _____

4. shipper: _____

   _____

5. colorless: _____

   _____

TIP: When you read, you may notice words with suffixes. If you remember what the suffix means, you may be able to figure out the meaning of a word.

Writing Activity   Write a short paragraph that correctly uses key vocabulary words to discuss the considerations involved in buying a motor scooter. Use at least four of the words from the list on page 75. Reread the definitions, if necessary.

_____

_____

_____

Think about your reading.

Check your comprehension.   Answer each question. If you don't know the answer, reread the lines in parentheses.

1. How is a motor scooter different from a moped? (lines 6–13)

   _____

2. What is legally required to drive a motor scooter? (lines 13–15)

   _____

3. Compare the gas mileage of an average scooter with a mileage for a car. (lines 30–32)

   _____

4. Why should people be cautious about buying motor scooters online? (lines 71–72)

   _____

Use reading skills: Classify information.

When you **classify** information, you sort it into different kinds or groups. In this article, you might classify the reasons to get or not get a scooter.

Classify information.   Reread this part of the article:

> Think about your commute. If you travel a long distance to work, much of it on highways, you may want the speed and protection a car offers. On the other hand, if you have a short commute and parking is an issue, a scooter may be an excellent choice since it is easy to maneuver and easy to park.

1. List the reasons for driving a car.

   _____

2. List the reasons for driving a moped.

   _____

Use a graphic organizer.

You can use a graphic organizer like the one below to help you classify information. Fill in the organizer with the pluses and minuses, the good and bad things, about a motor scooter.

Pluses (Good)	Minuses (Bad)

Write About It

Write a how-to paragraph.

Write a how-to paragraph telling someone how to buy a motor scooter. When you write a how-to paragraph, you tell how to do something. You will write the steps a person can take to successfully buy a motor scooter.

Prewriting   When you want to tell people how to do something step-by-step, a graphic organizer like this can be helpful. The first two steps are done for you. Fill in the other boxes with the rest of the steps a person who is buying a motor scooter should take. Write the steps in order.

1. Make sure you want a scooter and not a moped or motorcycle.

2. Decide if you want a new or used scooter.

Thinking Beyond Reading   Think about these questions and discuss them with a partner. Add ideas to the flow chart as you talk and think of additional steps.

• Should a person with a long commute buy a scooter?

• What could a person read to decide about buying a scooter?

• How would you decide if buying a scooter is economical for you?

Write a draft.   Write a first draft of your paragraph. Use the graphic organizer to help you write. Your paragraph might begin with a topic sentence like this: "If you want to buy a motor scooter, here's what you should do."

_____

_____

_____

_____

_____

_____

_____

_____

_____

_____

_____

_____

_____

Revise and create a final draft.   Write your final draft on a separate piece of paper. As you revise, check your draft for these specific points:

• Did you include steps to take to buy a motor scooter?

• Did you put the steps in order?

• Did you check to make sure that your spelling and punctuation are correct?

Food Facts

Learning Objectives

In this lesson you will:

▧ Learn about chocolate.

▧ Compare and contrast.

▧ Master the key vocabulary used in the article.

▧ Write an explanation of how chocolate is made.

Key Vocabulary

absorb *(verb)* to take something in through the surface

celebrated *(adjective)* famous or talked about a lot

debut *(noun)* first appearance

fashionable *(adjective)* following the latest styles

hardier *(adjective)* stronger and sturdier

hybrid *(noun)* a mixture of two or more different things

manufacturers *(noun)* companies that make goods, usually in large quantities

process *(noun)* a series of actions that someone does to achieve a certain result

surrounding *(adjective)* around, near

temperamental *(adjective)* hard to predict

Before You Read

Try these active reading strategies. They'll keep you more involved in the article. Decide what you want to learn from a reading so you can look for information as you read. Or ask yourself questions about what you're reading and try to find the answers as you read.

Use what you know.

1. What do you think chocolate is made of?

   _____

   _____

   _____

   _____

2. Tell about your favorite kinds of chocolate.

   _____

   _____

   _____

   _____

Ask yourself questions.

1. What would you like to know about the history of chocolate?

   _____

   _____

   _____

   _____

2. What would you like to learn about how chocolate is made?

   _____

   _____

   _____

   _____

Chocolate: Food of the Gods

How much do you know about chocolate? In this article you'll learn the secrets of chocolate's dark, delicious history. Underline or highlight the sentences that show the different countries involved in chocolate's history.

From candy to drinks, from ice cream to cookies, chocolate provides a quick energy burst or a comforting break. Some people call chocolate "the food of the gods."

A Short History of Chocolate

5 People in South America have been drinking chocolate since around 900 B.C. In 1519, explorers from Spain arrived in Mexico and drank chocolate for the first time. The drink they were served was a hot, bitter drink of chocolate mixed with water and spices such as cinnamon, chili pepper, and vanilla. The explorers brought the drink back to Spain where it was served
10 hot, sweetened, and with fewer spices.

Almost a hundred years later the French first tried—and got hooked on—the Spanish chocolate drink. Soon shops throughout Europe started serving hot chocolate to the rich. These shops became clubs where **fashionable** people talked politics. The English added milk to the hot drink in the early 1700s.
15 Beginning in 1765, sea captains started taking cacao beans to the American colonies. That's when chocolate candy made its **debut.** American **manufacturers** roasted the beans, ground them, and turned them into chocolate candy. At first they sold the candy only in the colonies. In the 1800s, they started selling chocolate candy to England where it quickly became
20 very popular. A Swiss man created a **process** to make milk chocolate candy bars in 1876.

cacao beans *(noun)*
the beans from which chocolate is made

Today the United States is the largest manufacturer of chocolate. Chocolate from around the world is **celebrated** for its different qualities.

1. How did chocolate get to Europe?

_____

_____

Did you know there are three kinds of cacao beans? When you read details about the three kinds of beans, make a check in the margin.

More About the Bean

25   There are three main kinds of cacao beans grown today. The most expensive beans come from Central America and the Caribbean islands. These beans are hard to grow and have an unusual, complex, and delicate taste. Less than five percent of the world's chocolate is made from these beans.

The second kind of cacao bean is grown widely in Africa. About two-thirds
30   of the world's cacao beans come from Africa. The trees these beans grow on are **hardier** than the trees that grow in Central America. The beans make a good everyday chocolate.

The third kind of cacao bean is a **hybrid** of the first two types. Trees with these beans were developed in Trinidad, an island in the Caribbean Sea.
35   Almost all chocolate manufactured today is made from cacao trees in either Africa or Trinidad.

People have tried to grow cacao trees in other places, but cacao trees are hard to grow. They grow only near the equator. The trees get damaged if the temperature drops below 60 degrees.
40   When the cacao beans are ready to harvest, the large pods are taken from the trees. The beans and their **surrounding** pulp are left to ferment for a week. This process helps create the chocolate taste. Then the beans (now called cocoa beans) are spread out in the sun to dry.

After the beans are dried, they are cleaned and roasted. They are also
45   graded for quality. The shells of the beans are thrown away, and the remainder is ground up. Grinding the beans releases the cocoa butter and produces chocolate liquor . At this point, the chocolate has formed a paste and is ready to be processed.

2. What is the rarest kind of cacao bean?

_____

_____

ferment *(verb)*
to cause a slow chemical change that breaks down complex substances into simpler substances

chocolate liquor *(noun)*
the liquid or paste that is produced when cacao beans are roasted and ground

3. What part of the process creates the chocolate taste?

_____

_____

Continue reading to find out how the bitter chocolate paste becomes the sweet stuff we love to eat. When you read a step in the process, number it in the margin.

From Bean to Chocolate

50   The chocolate paste is made into one of three products: unsweetened baking chocolate, cocoa powder, and chocolate candy. If the paste is made into a solid, it is sold as unsweetened baking chocolate. If the cocoa butter is removed from the paste, it is sold as cocoa powder. If sugar, flavorings, and additional cocoa butter are added, it is sold as chocolate candy.

55   There are three main kinds of chocolate candy. Dark chocolate contains sugar, chocolate liquor, and cocoa butter. Milk chocolate contains those same ingredients plus milk. White chocolate contains the same ingredients as milk chocolate minus the chocolate liquor. The finest dark chocolate has at least 70 percent chocolate liquor and cocoa butter. In general, the higher the

60 percentage, the finer the chocolate.

      To make chocolate candy, the sugar, cocoa, and milk are ground in a process called conching . The bits in the mixture are ground so finely that the tongue cannot feel them. That's what makes chocolate smooth. Then the chocolate is tempered , which means it is carefully melted and cooled. If

65 the melting temperature is too high, the chocolate may turn too hard. If the melting temperature is too low, the chocolate will be crumbly.

      Chocolate is **temperamental.** If it is stored at too cold a temperature, the fat and sugar rise to the top and the chocolate may turn white. If chocolate is stored with other foods, it can **absorb** their smells.

70   The melting point of chocolate is just below normal human temperature. That's one of the reasons so many people love the taste and feel of chocolate melting on the tongue. Scientists say that the chemicals in chocolate make people happy—but most of us don't need scientists to tell us that.

conching *(noun)*
    a grinding process used to make chocolate

tempered *(adjective)*
    gradually heated and then cooled

4. What three basic products can chocolate paste be made into?

_____

_____

5. Describe chocolate after it is conched.

_____

_____

After You Read

Build a robust vocabulary.

Writing Sentences   Write a complete sentence to respond to each of the following questions or statements. Use the underlined word in your answer. Use the definitions on page 85 to help you.

1. Name a <u>hybrid</u> car.

    _____

2. Name a <u>celebrated</u> actor.

    _____

3. What is a <u>temperamental</u> person like?

    _____

4. What do <u>manufacturers</u> of candy bars do?

    _____

5. Name a <u>process</u>.

    _____

Sentence Completions   Complete each sentence using a word from the box.

absorb	celebrated	debut	fashionable	hardier
hybrid	manufacturers	process	surrounding	temperamental

1. That new adventure movie is making its _____ next week.

2. Drinking chocolate was once a _____ activity for rich people in France.

3. A sponge will _____ water.

4. Because that kind of tree is _____ than most, it grows well in cold temperatures.

5. There is a covering of white chocolate _____ the dark chocolate.

Word Building   A **root word** is the main part of a word that contains its basic meaning. For example, the word *happy* is the root word in *unhappiness.* If you recognize the parts of a word, it is easier to figure out what a new word means.

Look at the following sentence from the article.

> These shops became clubs where fashionable people talked politics.

Circle the root word in *shops, clubs, fashionable,* and *talked.* Check your answers with a partner.

Read these words. Circle the root word in each. Then write another word that uses the same root word. Use that new word in a sentence.

1. surrounding: _____

_____

2. overdo: _____

_____

3. reconnect: _____

_____

4. illegal: _____

_____

5. presentation: _____

_____

TIP: Look for the root word within words you don't know. For example, if you know the word *triangle* means "a figure with three sides," you might be able to tell that *triangular* means "having three sides."

Writing Activity Write a short paragraph that correctly uses key vocabulary words to tell about part of the history of chocolate. Use at least four of the words from the list on page 85. Reread the definitions, if necessary.

_____

_____

_____

Think about your reading.

Check your comprehension. Answer each question. If you don't know the answer, reread the lines in parentheses.

1. When did chocolate candy become popular in England? (lines 18–20)

_____

2. What are the three places where cacao beans are grown? (lines 25–36)

_____

3. What are the three main kinds of chocolate candy? (lines 55–58)

_____

4. How is chocolate tempered? (lines 63–64)

_____

Use reading skills: Compare and contrast.

When you **compare** pieces of information, you decide what is the same about them. When you **contrast** pieces of information, you decide what is different about them. In this article, you can compare and contrast hot chocolate and chocolate candy.

Compare and contrast.   In this article, you can also compare and contrast different kinds of eating-chocolate. Reread this part of the article:

> There are three main kinds of chocolate candy. Dark chocolate contains sugar, chocolate liquor, and cocoa butter. Milk chocolate contains those same ingredients plus milk. White chocolate contains the same ingredients as milk chocolate minus the chocolate liquor. The finest dark chocolate has at least 70 percent chocolate liquor and cocoa butter. In general, the higher the percentage, the finer the chocolate.

1.   How are the three kinds of chocolate alike?

_____

_____

2.   How are the three kinds of chocolate different?

_____

_____

Use a graphic organizer.

You can use a graphic organizer like the Venn diagram below to help you compare and contrast information. Fill in the diagram to show what is the same and what is different between two different kinds of cacao beans.

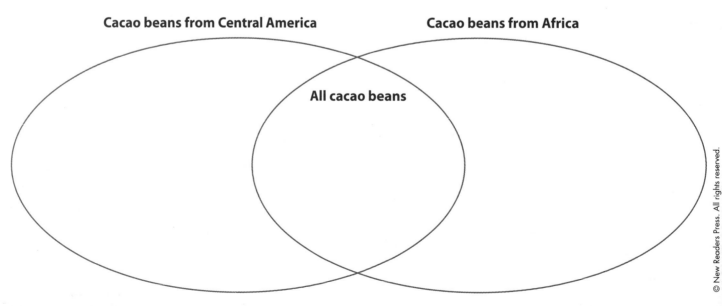

Cacao beans from Central America   **Cacao beans from Africa**

All cacao beans

Write About It

Write an explanation.

You often want to explain something when you write. Write a paragraph that explains how chocolate is made from cacao beans. This kind of explanation describes a process, so you will want to list the steps in order.

Prewriting   You can use the flowchart below to help you write the steps for making chocolate candy. This will be a helpful outline for your writing. Work on your own or with a partner.

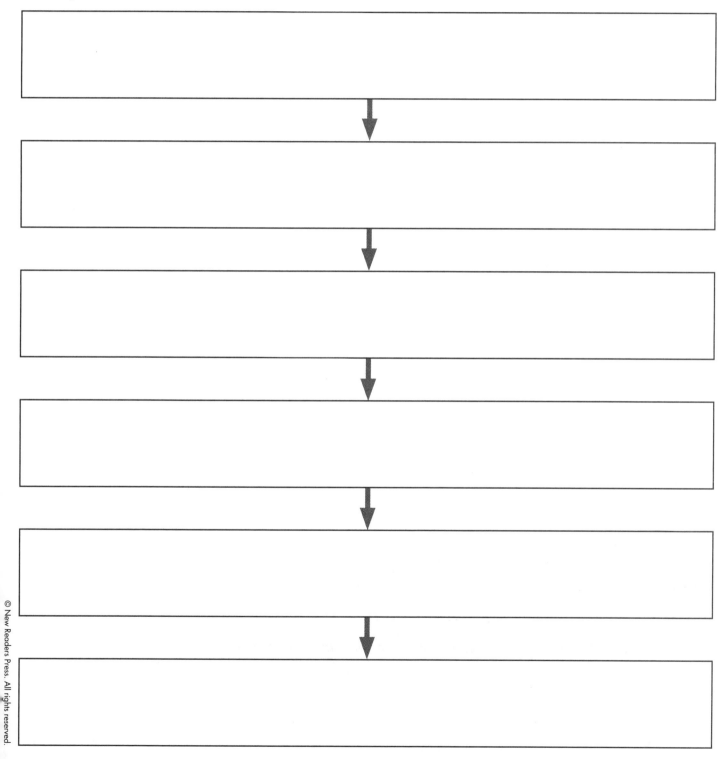

Thinking Beyond Reading   Think about these questions and discuss them with a partner. Add ideas to the flowchart as you talk and think of additional steps.

- Could cacao beans be grown in other parts of the world?

- Why is it important to grade cacao beans for quality?

- Why is the United States such a big producer of chocolate?

Write a draft.   Write a first draft of your explanation. Use the flowchart you wrote as an outline. Your paragraph might begin with a topic sentence like this: "When you make chocolate, you start with raw cacao beans."

_____

_____

_____

_____

_____

_____

_____

_____

_____

_____

_____

_____

_____

Revise and create a final draft.   Write your final draft on a separate piece of paper. As you revise, check your draft for these specific points:

- Did you include all the important steps in making chocolate?

- Does the explanation move smoothly from step to step?

- Did you check spelling and grammar to make sure your writing is clear and correct?

Being Your Own Boss

Learning Objectives

In this lesson you will:

▨ Read a story about a woman's experience with yard sales.

▨ Identify cause and effect.

▨ Master the key vocabulary used in the story.

▨ Write a summary of the story.

Key Vocabulary

anxiously *(adverb)* in an uneasy or worried way

devised *(verb)* worked out; thought up

hustled *(verb)* worked energetically

improvised *(adjective)* made of whatever was at hand

makeshift *(adjective)* used for a while in place of the real thing

ridiculously *(adverb)* foolishly

satisfaction *(noun)* a pleasant feeling of having everything that you need or want, or of reaching success in something

theme *(noun)* the main idea of something

thrived *(verb)* grew very well

wince *(verb)* to draw back suddenly

Before You Read

As you begin to read this story, think of questions you want answered as you read. You will probably want to know first what the title means. Continue asking yourself questions and looking for the answers as you read. As an active reader, you can also stop during reading to summarize what you have read up to that point in the story.

Ask yourself questions.

1. What do you think "glitter" and "cash" will have to do with this story?

   _____

   _____

   _____

   _____

Brenda seems happy about the yard sale she wants to hold. Will it be successful?

2. Read the first four paragraphs of the story. What do you want to know about the sale Brenda is planning?

   _____

   _____

   _____

   _____

   _____

Summarize what you read.

1. Summarize what happens in the beginning of the story when Brenda and George talk.

   _____

   _____

   _____

   _____

To summarize this first part of the story, I have to understand the main things that happen when Brenda and George talk to each other.

Glitter and Cash

Read the story to find out how a woman plans a yard sale—and gets much more than she bargained for. Highlight or mark the steps Brenda goes through to prepare for the yard sale.

Brenda looked around the basement and sighed. Junk everywhere. TVs from the Ice Age. Spangles from a long-ago party. An old sifter. She was sitting in the middle of the mess when George came in.

"OK," Brenda said, her chin in her hand. "Now, I'm officially discouraged. I
5 thought cleaning up this mess would be easier."

George looked around as he took bites from his apple. "Easy, babe," he said. "Yard sale."

Brenda looked at George as if he'd just given her a kiss. "Good one. That's it. An ad in the paper, some big bright orange signs, and we're in business. Two
10 weekends from now. You rock, George."

The hauling and tagging and sorting took days, but with the thought of cash in sight, the job was bearable. Then Brenda's friends started calling. She did have a great location, right on a busy street. Their friends also brought over tons of their junk, and some nicer stuff, too. Brenda **devised** a color-coded
15 tagging system. Then she got creative, putting all the vintage clothing together in an **improvised** tent, hanging the pots and pans from hooks in the trees. "Looks pretty good if I do say so," Brenda thought to herself with **satisfaction.**

The yard sale was an over-the-top success. By the time all the crowds had
20 left, there was little left but a few crumpled red and purple tags—and a bag full of money. Her friends were thrilled, too. "How'd you get so much for this junk?" one asked, fanning out the money Brenda had given her.

vintage *(adjective)*
  from an earlier time

Brenda shrugged. "I knew one of the dresses you were selling was a well-known '60s designer," she said, "so I priced it higher. A lady came by who was looking for vintage clothing, and she snapped it up—full price."

"You should think about doing this again," her friend Tawna said. "I'll even pay you a commission ."

1. Why is Brenda unhappy as she looks around the basement?

_____

2. How does Brenda get the idea to have a yard sale?

_____

Brenda seems to like this yard sale business. Ask yourself a question about what will happen next? Underline the sentences that answer your question.

Tawna's comment rolled around in Brenda's mind for days. She even went back to the basement to see if there was anything she'd overlooked the first time, and decided there was. Brenda decided that if she were going to do this again, she was going to do a better job. She spent the next few weekends on scouting trips to yard sales, thrift shops, and secondhand stores. She picked up ideas for how to price things. She bought at a yard sale an armful of 1960s clothes that were **ridiculously** underpriced, and then did the same thing at a dusty thrift shop where everything was jammed together on wire racks. She learned to return to garage sales late on Sunday afternoons—if anything was left and was worth buying, it could be bought for almost nothing.

Brenda went back to Tawna. "Were you serious about the commission?" she asked.

"I was," Tawna nodded. "You really know what you're doing, and it's a lot of work. I'd happily give you a commission."

Tawna spread the word. So did Brenda, although she was uncomfortable telling friends they needed to pay her. The friends didn't seem to mind, though—they felt the same way Tawna did. Brenda would be doing the work, and she deserved something for her efforts.

"You've got a real feel for this business," Jody, a friend of Tawna's, said as she handed over a pile of clothes and took a receipt . "I saw that stuff you had at the first sale. You've got a good eye."

Brenda had her next sale a month and a half later. This time, she used a spreadsheet to help her keep track of what she had. Brenda set up the sale like a store. She even set up a **makeshift** dressing room.

The second sale was an even bigger smash. Friends who had been at the first one told other friends. The special vintage clothing section that Brenda set up was empty by 2:30 on Saturday afternoon. At the end, Brenda sat back, too tired for words, and counted her profits. She was amazed. Even with the

commission (noun)
part of the money from a sale given to the person who makes the sale

receipt (noun)
a written statement that money or things have been received

spreadsheet (noun)
a chart with information in rows and columns

costs of picking up some merchandise at other sales, she had made a lot of money.

merchandise *(noun)*
goods that are bought or sold

3. Why does Brenda visit other yard sales?

_____

4. Why is Tawna willing to give Brenda a commission?

_____

What will Brenda do next? Write your idea on a sticky note. Then add a check mark if your idea is correct.

60   Weeks after the second sale was over, Brenda kept getting calls from people wanting to know when she would have the next one. By then, Brenda had a new idea. She wanted to start a shop.

"I've got the place all picked out," she told Tawna. "On Broadway where all those other funky stores are. I can afford the rent with the money I saved for the new car I was going to buy. What do you think?"

65   "Brilliant," Tawna said. "What's the name? What's your **theme?** How's it going to be different from the other stores around there?"

"Since the stuff I have is mostly '60s, I thought about calling it Groovy. What do you think? Does it make you **wince?**" Brenda said **anxiously.**

"No, I like it," Tawna said, nodding. "I like it. And you should do it. Definitely."

70   Brenda planned carefully. She haunted thrift shops and yard sales and built up her inventory . She put the word out to friends that she was buying anything they had from the 1960s, or that had a 1960s feeling. And six months later, after planning, painting, buying stationery, and talking to credit card companies, she was ready to open.

inventory *(noun)*
a list of goods or items

75   After the grand opening, when her friends came and dragged their friends along, there was a drop in sales. Brenda panicked. Then she got out and **hustled.** She got a spot on a local TV show talking up her new store. She printed flyers and left them in clubs. She got a reporter from the local free weekly newspaper to write a story. And it all worked. Word got around, and

80   the little yard sale that became a store **thrived.** Brenda was her own boss. She was making money. Everything was Groovy.

5. Why does Brenda pick the location she does for her shop?

_____

6. Why does Brenda name her shop Groovy?

_____

After You Read

Build a robust vocabulary.

Writing Sentences   Write a complete sentence to respond to each of the following questions. Use the underlined word in your answer. Use the definitions on page 95 to help you.

1. What is an example of something with a <u>theme</u>?

   _____

2. What might make you <u>wince</u>?

   _____

3. What gives you <u>satisfaction</u>?

   _____

4. What have you made that was <u>improvised</u>?

   _____

5. What might you do <u>anxiously</u>?

   _____

Sentence Completions   Complete each sentence using a word from the box.

anxiously	**devised**	**hustled**	**improvised**	**makeshift**
ridiculously	**satisfaction**	**theme**	**thrived**	**wince**

1. Brenda _____ a tagging system for the items she was selling.

2. The shop _____ after Brenda made sure people knew about it.

3. The _____ dressing room allowed people to try on clothes at the yard sale.

4. Brenda _____ to find great things to sell at her store.

5. Some of the things Brenda found at yard sales were _____ cheap.

Word Building   A **suffix** is a group of letters added to the end of a word. When you add a suffix you form a new word with a new meaning. The suffix *-ist* can describe what someone does. An *artist* is someone who makes art. The suffix *-ful* means "full of something." The word *hopeful* means full of hope.

Write the definition of each word. Use the meaning of the suffix to help you figure out what the word means. Then use each word in a sentence.

1. machinist: _____

_____

2. harmful: _____

_____

3. flavorful: _____

_____

4. biologist: _____

_____

TIP: Look for suffixes in words when you read. If you know what the suffix means, you can probably figure out the meaning of the word.

Writing Activity   Write a short paragraph that correctly uses key vocabulary words to tell about Brenda getting her store ready. Use at least four of the words from the list on page 95. Reread the definitions, if necessary.

_____

_____

_____

_____

Think about your reading.

Check your comprehension.   Answer each question. If you don't know the answer, reread the lines in parentheses.

1. How well did Brenda's first yard sale go? (lines 19–21)

_____

2. Why was Brenda amazed after the second yard sale? (lines 55–57)

_____

3. What does Brenda sell in her shop? (line 66)

_____

4. Where does Brenda find things to sell in her shop? (lines 70–72)

_____

Use reading skills: Identify cause and effect.

Causes are why things happen. **Effects** are what happens as a result of something else. In the story you have just read, many of Brenda's actions are a result of other actions or events.

Identify cause and effect.   Reread this section of the story to find the causes and the effects.

> Brenda had her next sale a month and a half later. This time, she used a spreadsheet to help her keep track of what she had. Brenda set up the sale like a store. She even set up a makeshift dressing room.
>
> The second sale was an even bigger smash. Friends who had been at the first one told other friends. The special vintage clothing section that Brenda set up was empty by 2:30 on Saturday afternoon. At the end, Brenda sat back, too tired for words, and counted her profits. She was amazed. Even with the costs of picking up some merchandise at other sales, she had made a lot of money.

1.   What causes the second garage sale to be such a success?

_____

_____

_____

2.   What is the effect of Brenda working very hard on the second sale?

_____

_____

_____

Use a graphic organizer.

You can use a graphic organizer like the one below to understand the causes and the effects of other actions or events. Fill in the boxes to help you think about the events in the story.

Cause	Effect
Brenda has stuff from the basement she wants to clear out.	1.
Brenda scouts other yard sales and thrift shops for merchandise for the second sale.	2.
3.	Brenda's store is a huge success.

Write About It

Write a summary.

Write a one-paragraph summary of this story. When you write a summary, you include only the most important information. In a story like this, a summary would include only the most important events. For example, you probably would include George's suggestion that Brenda hold a garage sale, but you probably would not include what is in Brenda's basement.

Prewriting When you write a summary of a story, you might want to fill out a graphic organizer in which you write phrases that tell the most important things that happen in the story. The first one is already done for you. Work on your own or with a partner to fill in the rest of the chart. Add more boxes if you need them.

Brenda decides to clean out her basement.

↓

↓

↓

↓

↓

Thinking Beyond Reading   Think about these questions and discuss them with a partner. Add ideas to the graphic organizer as you talk.

- Have you listed the most important ideas in the story?

- Have you organized events in the order that they happened?

- Have you included any unnecessary details that should be removed?

Write a draft.   Write a first draft of your summary. Use the graphic organizer to help you. Your summary might begin like this: "When the story begins, Brenda wants to clean out her basement."

_____

_____

_____

_____

_____

_____

_____

_____

_____

_____

_____

_____

_____

_____

Revise and create a final draft.   Write your final draft on a separate piece of paper. As you revise, check your draft for these specific points:

- Did you include all the important events that happened in the story?

- Did you put the events in order?

- Did you check to make sure your spelling and punctuation are correct?

Answer Key

Lesson 1 You Can Save Your Own Life
pp. 5–14

Writing Sentences

Sample answers:

1. The heart is an <u>internal</u> organ.

2. Two <u>symptoms</u> of a stroke are paralysis and feeling confused.

3. Losing interest in eating is a sign of <u>depression</u>.

4. I might <u>hesitate</u> before speaking if I wasn't sure of the answer.

5. I felt <u>confused</u> the first time I took the subway.

Sentence Completions

1. spasm
2. reluctance
3. permanent
4. decipher
5. digestion

Word Building

Underline *heat, forget, fool, staple, wise.*

Sample answers:

1. reusing: Reusing plastic bags is good for the environment.

2. rejoin: I decided to rejoin the gym because I want to keep fit.

3. sleeping: I have trouble sleeping on hot nights.

4. preview: If you preview the movie, you will know what your kids will be watching.

5. helpful: The receptionist at the doctor's office was very helpful.

Writing Activity

Answers will vary. Review the vocabulary words and the definitions. Find the words in the article to make sure they are used correctly.

Check your comprehension.

Sample answers:

1. Sudden weight loss can be a sign of cancer, depression, or AIDS.

2. You should see a doctor when the pain lasts several months, if the pain is very bad, or if you can't eat.

3. You should see a doctor if you have a headache with a stiff neck because you might have meningitis.

4. The signs of a stroke are slurred speech, paralysis, tingling, and confusion.

Identify fact and opinion.

Sample answers:

1. Fact: If you have black stools, you could have bleeding problems or cancer.

2. Opinion: It may be difficult to talk about stools, but it's a lot more difficult to deal with cancer.

Use a graphic organizer.

Sample answers:

Facts:

An aneurysm is a weak spot in an artery wall that can kill you.

If you have a stiff neck along with your headache, it may mean that you have meningitis.

Meningitis is a serious infection.

Opinions:

We all get headaches.

Headaches are no fun.

You should trust yourself.

Prewriting

Answers will vary but might include: see a doctor if I have stomach pain for a long time, see a doctor if I have the signs of a stroke, see a doctor if my body just doesn't feel right.

Thinking Beyond Reading

The graphic organizer might now include more ways you can take responsibility for your own health.

Write a draft.

Your first draft might begin by summing up your main point. Include the supporting points you wrote in your graphic organizer.

Revise and create a final draft.

Your final draft should include a topic sentence and details to support the main idea. The paragraph should have few grammatical and spelling errors.

Lesson 2 Getting Along at Work
pp. 15–24

Writing Sentences

Sample answers:

1. Sometimes I feel <u>frustration</u> trying to balance my checkbook.

2. <u>Insincerity</u> is telling someone you like what they're wearing when you don't.

3. Two people might call a <u>truce</u> if they've been arguing.

4. I <u>stifled</u> an angry reply to someone who was rude.

5. A house on fire needs <u>urgent</u> action.

Sentence Completions

1. sarcastically
2. maneuvering
3. caressed
4. ingratiating
5. efficient

Word Building

Circle *under-, non-, micro-,* and *under-.*

Sample answers:

1. microphone: Speak into the microphone.

2. nonalcoholic: We serve only nonalcoholic drinks.

3. undercover: The police officers were working undercover.

4. underage: Underage people are not allowed into the club.

5. nonsense: Everything he said was nonsense.

Writing Activity

Answers will vary. Review the vocabulary words and the definitions. Find the words in the story to see how they are used.

Check your comprehension.

Sample answers:

1. Al dislikes his boss because he thinks his boss picks on him for no reason.

2. Al keeps his temper and tells Steve he'll try harder.

3. Ben is a co-worker of Al's who has worked there a long time.

4. Al is happy at the end of the story because he thinks Steve will treat him fairly now.

Make judgments.

Sample answer:

My judgment is that Al did the right thing in the way he handled the conflict with his boss. He needs to keep his job, and the boss might fire him if he talks back.

Use a graphic organizer.

Sample answers:

1. Al did the right thing because he needs to keep the job.

2. Al is taking a chance, but it might make things better so it seems worth doing.

Prewriting

Answers will vary but may include: Al keeps his temper when his boss baits him. Al decides to be extra nice to Steve. Al knocks over goods with the forklift and Steve yells at him, but Al keeps his cool. Ben tells Al that Steve may resent Al because Steve lost his younger brother who was about the same age as Al. Al talks to Steve about his brother and makes friends with him.

Thinking Beyond Reading

The graphic organizer should include only the main characters in the story, only important details, and the fact that Al worked out his problems with his boss.

Write a draft.

Use the details in your chart to help you write.

Revise and create a final draft.

The final draft should include the important events in the story in the order that they occurred. Sentences should be complete and use correct spelling and punctuation.

Lesson 3 The Changing Family
pp. 25–34

Writing Sentences

Sample answers:

1. A <u>self-sufficient</u> person can take care of herself.

2. I felt <u>resentful</u> when my brother wrecked my car, but didn't want to pay for it.

3. The <u>population</u> of my town is about 25,000.

4. My <u>responsibilities</u> include doing the dishes and doing the laundry.

5. My grandmother <u>nurtured</u> me when I was a child.

Sentence Completions

1. reversal
2. increasingly
3. circumstances
4. martyr
5. phenomenon

Word Building

Circle *-ment* in each word.

Sample answers:

1. I knew there would be an improvement in my test scores because I had studied so hard.

2. He had his retirement party when he was 65.

Writing Activity

Answers will vary. Review the vocabulary words and the definitions. Find the words in the article to make sure they are used correctly.

Check your comprehension.

Sample answers:

1. The number of people in the sandwich generation is growing because people are living longer due to better living conditions and health care.

2. You can visit them and check to see if there is fresh food in the refrigerator, the house is clean, and the bills are paid.

3. You can call the state's general help number.

4. You should talk to your children about the changes, their concerns, and their new responsibilities if they will have any.

Synthesize information.

Sample answer:

The sandwich generation is made up of people who have responsibility for both younger and older family members.

Use a graphic organizer.

Sample answers:

Bring things from their home.

Remember to take care of yourself.

Make your home safe.

Synthesis: You need to think of everyone who will live together in the house before your parents move in.

Prewriting

Answers will vary but may include: Help them with their finances, Keep other family members involved, Check in to see how they are doing, Find help within the family, Go with them to the doctor.

Thinking Beyond Reading

Answers will vary, but the graphic organizer might now include additional information.

Write a draft.

Your first draft might begin by summing up the main point of the paragraph. Include the supporting points you wrote in your graphic organizer.

Revise and create a final draft.

The paragraph should include a topic sentence and details to support the main idea. The paragraph should have few grammatical and spelling errors.

Lesson 4 Keeping Neighborhoods Safe pp. 35–44

Writing Sentences

Sample answers:

1. You can give people good reasons to join, but you can't <u>ensure</u> that they will join.

2. An example of <u>suspicious</u> behavior is someone who wanders around looking nervous and out of place.

3. You can <u>persuade</u> people by telling them about crime in the neighborhood.

4. An <u>epidemic</u> of burglaries is a large number of burglaries.

5. You can <u>expand</u> a Neighborhood Watch by holding a community barbecue.

Sentence Completions

1. address
2. organizational
3. efficiently
4. initiative
5. cohesive

Word Building

Sample answers:

1. jumped: The child jumped off the steps.

2. mopped: We mopped the floors before the party.

3. tamed: The animal handler tamed the wild cats.

4. filled: Marta filled her cup with coffee.

5. flipped: We flipped a coin to see who would go first.

Writing Activity

Answers will vary. Review the vocabulary words and the definitions. Find the words in the article to see how they are used.

Check your comprehension.

Sample answers:

1. The local law enforcement people will have materials to distribute and might speak to the group at the meeting.

2. A flyer should include place, date, time, what will happen at the meeting, and what a Neighborhood Watch is.

3. Knowing neighbors can keep crime down because people know when something doesn't seem right.

4. A safe network usually has signs in houses that show children those are safe houses to go to for help.

Draw conclusions.

Sample answers:

1. I learned to ask in person to persuade people to come.

2. I know my neighborhood has people who are concerned about crime.

3. I would ask people personally and tell them this is a way to reduce crime.

Use a graphic organizer.

Sample answers:

1. What You Know: My local police station seems like a friendly place.

   Conclusion You Draw: If I went to the police station, the people there would probably help me with the watch.

2. What You Know: People are worried they'll have to do too much.

   Conclusion You Draw: If we tell people that each committee will only do one job, people will be more interested.

3. What You Know: My community likes picnics.

   Conclusion You Draw: If we had a Neighborhood Watch, a picnic would help people in the group get to know each other.

Prewriting

Answers will vary but may include: Time of meeting, place of meeting, what will happen at the meeting, and what a Neighborhood Watch is.

Thinking Beyond Reading

Answers to the questions might include: A Neighborhood Watch group could be successful in a place where criminals know everyone is watching; communities where people are constantly moving might not be good for a Neighborhood Watch group; a good leader should be a good listener.

Write a draft.

Use the details in your chart to help you write your letter. Follow the letter form.

Revise and create a final draft.

The final draft should include all the information someone would need to come to the meeting. Sentences should be complete and use correct spelling and punctuation.

Lesson 5 Everyone Can Read
pp. 45–54

Writing Sentences

Sample answers:

1. If you <u>descend</u> a hill, you're at the bottom when you finish.

2. I'm <u>proficient</u> at fixing cars.

3. I have <u>enthusiasm</u> for the New York Mets.

4. You might leave a place <u>abruptly</u> if you see someone you don't want to talk to.

5. If you don't have the right <u>specifications</u>, the tires won't fit.

Sentence Completions

1. despair

2. impatiently

3. inspiration

4. foreboding

5. floundering

Word Building

Circle *men, women.*

1. e

2. a

3. d

4. c

5. b

Sample answers:

1. There are 12 people in our class.

2. Bob and Judy have six children.

3. All the women in my family are short.

Writing Activity

Answers will vary. Review the vocabulary words and the definitions. Find the words in the story to make sure they are used correctly.

Check your comprehension.

Sample answers:

1. He had to read an instruction manual at work.

2. Cal felt that the people in the classroom all shared a look of defeat.

3. Improving his reading helped Cal become more confident.

4. Because she changed his life.

Compare and contrast.

Sample answers:

1. Cal works on the assembly line.

2. At the beginning Cal is terrified that people might discover he can't read well. At the end of the story he is confident.

Use a graphic organizer.

Sample answers:

At work: Can be boring, Memos

Both: Black and white, Not too long, Some pictures

At home: Interesting, Newspaper, Fiction

Prewriting

Sample answers:

Cal before: Felt like a failure, Was scared when he had to read.

Same: Good at his work, Smart

Cal after: Confident, Feels better about himself, Can read well

Thinking Beyond Reading

Answers will vary, but the graphic organizer might now include more information about Cal.

Write a draft.

Your first draft might begin by summing up the main point of the paragraph. Include the supporting points you wrote in your graphic organizer.

Revise and create a final draft.

The paragraph should include a topic sentence and details to support the main idea. The paragraph should have few grammatical and spelling errors.

Lesson 6 A Crime-Fighting Agency pp. 55–64

Writing Sentences

Sample answers:

1. A gun law could be <u>controversial</u> because people don't agree about guns.

2. <u>Technicians</u> in a crime lab might study DNA samples.

3. My <u>priorities</u> for today are to clean the house and finish my school work.

4. In my family, my husband has the <u>responsibility</u> for cooking.

5. A painting could have an <u>intricate</u> design.

Sentence Completions

1. preoccupation
2. technology
3. enduring
4. infiltrated
5. ruthless

Word Building

high/way, bullet/proof, paper/back, law/maker, court/house

Sample answers:

1. I'll buy a paperback book.

2. You can renew your driver's license at the courthouse.

Writing Activity

Answers will vary. Review the vocabulary words and the definitions. Find the words in the article to see how they are used.

Check your comprehension.

Sample answers:

1. The FBI was controversial at first because people thought local police should solve crimes.

2. The FBI's main interest in the 1940s was catching spies.

3. The FBI gets involved with crimes that can damage computers and computer thefts of money and identity.

4. The FBI crime lab works with DNA and fingerprints.

Identify main idea and details.

Sample answers:

1. The main idea of the section is that even though there are many things people have to do to qualify to work for the FBI, people want to do it.

2. Agents must have college degrees; they must be certain ages; they must agree to work as agents for three years.

Use a graphic organizer.

Sample answers:

terrorism; spies; financial crime; computer crime; crimes across state lines

Prewriting

Answers will vary but might include when the FBI began, what it does, how it has changed over the years, requirements for agents.

Thinking Beyond Reading

Answers to the questions might include: Americans think the FBI is very good at solving crimes; the role of the FBI changes depending on what people think is most important; people still want to be FBI agents because it is exciting work.

Write a draft.

Use the details in your chart to help you write.

Revise and create a final draft.

The final draft should include the main points of the article and the details that support them. Sentences should be complete and use correct spelling and punctuation.

Lesson 7 Opportunities Lost and Found pp. 65–74

Writing Sentences

Sample answers:

1. My younger brother can be an <u>annoyance</u> at times.

2. I felt <u>startled</u> when my friends threw me a surprise birthday party.

3. I look <u>disheveled</u> after I take a run.

4. If you speak <u>explosively</u>, you are speaking in a burst of energy.

5. I think Tiger Woods is a sports <u>phenomenon</u>.

Sentence Completions

1. pirouette	4. humility
2. incubator	5. deflated
3. desperation	

Word Building

Underline *un-, mis-, pre-, -over-*.

1. over	4. mis
2. un	5. over
3. pre	

Writing Activity

Answers will vary. Review the vocabulary words and the definitions. Find the words in the story to make sure they are used correctly.

Check your comprehension.

Sample answers:

1. Friz is thought to be a "has-been" because he could not play college basketball after getting a DUI.

2. They never asked him.

3. He thought it was his last chance to make the NBA.

4. T.J. had to decide if he would take his best shot or miss on purpose in order to help his brother.

Make inferences.

Sample answers:

1. Friz thinks this tournament might be the break he needs to have a career in the NBA.

2. The Rockets and Monarchs are both good teams.

3. T.J. is still a good player.

Use a graphic organizer.

Sample answers:

What you know: Sometimes people try to make their best shots and still don't make them.

Inference: T.J. may have been trying to make the shot and just missed.

Prewriting

Answers will vary but may include: The game started with Friz on a run; The Monarchs caught up; At the end of the game it was the Rockets up by 2 points; Friz's brother T.J. missed the last shot; The Rockets won.

Thinking Beyond Reading

Answers will vary, but the graphic organizer might now include more details.

Write a draft.

Your first draft might begin by summing up the main point of the story. Include the supporting points you wrote in your graphic organizer.

Revise and create a final draft.

The paragraph should include a topic sentence and details to support the main idea. The paragraph should have few grammatical and spelling errors.

Lesson 8 Traveling on Two Wheels pp. 75–84

Writing Sentences

Sample answers:

1. A convertible is a car with a top that can go down.

2. Air pollution is an environmental problem.

3. A residential area is where people's homes are found.

4. Yes, I'm good with mechanical things.

5. An inferior bike might cost less because it is made of cheaper materials.

Sentence Completions

1. impact	4. complexity
2. alternative	5. maneuver
3. consideration	

Word Building

Sample answers:

1. one who plays; Fred is a good pool player.

2. without a home; What can we do to help the homeless?

3. one who collects things; My friend is an art collector.

4. one who ships things; We'll use an overnight shipper to get the package there on time.

5. without color; The desert looked dry and colorless.

Writing Activity

Answers will vary. Review the vocabulary words and the definitions. Find the words in the article to see how they are used.

Check your comprehension.

Sample answers:

1. A moped is a motorized bike that goes more slowly than a motor scooter.

2. In most places you need a motorcycle license to drive a motor scooter.

3. Scooters get about 60–100 miles to a gallon of gas, while cars might get 20 miles to a gallon of gas.

4. Motor scooters bought through the Internet might be bad ones, so people should be cautious about buying them.

Classify information.

Sample answers:

1. Speed and protection when driving long distances and on highways

2. Easy to maneuver and park when a commute is short and parking is a problem

Use a graphic organizer.

Sample answers:

Pluses: costs less, gets better gas mileage, smaller environmental impact

Minuses: no protection from weather, not good for long commutes or highways

Prewriting

Answers will vary but may include the following: check if scooter requires adding oil with gas or not; decide if you want low or higher power; research if scooter is from well-known company and has good warranty. The steps should be numbered.

Thinking Beyond Reading

Answers to the questions might include: a person with a long commute on highways might be better off with something besides a scooter; could read driver magazine articles, also on the internet; have to do a budget with costs and use of gas, other expenses related to owning a vehicle, such as insurance.

Write a draft.

Use the details in your chart to help you write.

Revise and create a final draft.

The final draft should include the steps to take to buy a scooter, in order. Sentences should be complete and use correct spelling and punctuation.

Lesson 9 Food Facts
pp. 85–94

Writing Sentences

Sample answers:

1. A Prius is a <u>hybrid</u> car.

2. Tom Hanks is a <u>celebrated</u> actor.

3. You never know how a <u>temperamental</u> person will act.

4. <u>Manufacturers</u> of candy bars make candy bars.

5. Writing is a <u>process</u>.

Sentence Completions

1. debut

2. fashionable

3. absorb

4. hardier

5. surrounding

Word Building

Circle *shop, club, fashion, talk.*

Sample answers:

1. Circle *surround.*
   surrounded: Our house is surrounded by trees.

2. Circle *do.*
   doing: What are you doing tonight?

3. Circle *connect.*
   disconnected: Will disconnected his phone last night.

4. Circle *legal.*
   paralegal: Susan has a job as a paralegal.

5. Circle *present.*
   presented: The company presented Jake with a gold watch when he retired.

Writing Activity

Answers will vary. Review the vocabulary words and the definitions. Find the words in the article to make sure they are used correctly.

Check your comprehension.

Sample answers:

1. Chocolate candy became popular in England in the 1800s.

2. Cacao beans are grown in Trinidad, Africa, and Central America.

3. The three main kinds of eating-chocolate are milk, dark, and white.

4. Chocolate is tempered by heating it and cooling it.

Compare and contrast.

Sample answers:

1. They are sweet, they are for eating, and they contain sugar and cocoa butter.

2. Some have milk and some don't, and they have different percentages of chocolate liquor and cocoa butter.

Use a graphic organizer.

Sample answers:

Cacao beans from Central America: Rare, Taste complex.

All: Cacao beans grow on trees, Used to make chocolate.

Cacao beans from Africa: Most of the cacao beans in world, Everyday chocolate.

Prewriting

Answers will vary but may include: The beans are harvested and dried; Beans are roasted and ground; Sugar and flavorings are added; It's conched; It's tempered.

Thinking Beyond Reading

Answers may vary, but there might now be more steps in the graphic organizer.

Write a draft.

Your first draft might begin by summing up the main point of the paragraph. Include the supporting points you wrote in your graphic organizer.

Revise and create a final draft.

The paragraph should include a topic sentence and details to support the main idea. The paragraph should have few grammatical and spelling errors.

Lesson 10 Being Your Own Boss
pp. 95–104

Writing Sentences

Sample answers:

1. My daughter's birthday party had a princess <u>theme</u>.

2. A bad smell might make me <u>wince</u>.

3. Eating a good meal gives me <u>satisfaction</u>.

4. I used a plastic bag to make an <u>improvised</u> raincoat.

5. I drive <u>anxiously</u> on icy roads.

Sentence Completions

1. devised

2. thrived

3. makeshift or improvised

4. hustled

5. ridiculously

Word Building

Sample answers:

1. someone who uses machines; The machinist made the parts we needed.

2. full of harm; Keep harmful things away from children.

3. full of flavor; Sam cooks with flavorful spices.

4. someone who works in biology; My brother is a biologist.

Writing Activity

Answers will vary. Review the vocabulary words and the definitions. Find the words in the story to see how they are used.

Check your comprehension.

Sample answers:

1. The first yard sale went very well.

2. Brenda was amazed at how much money she made.

3. Brenda sells things from the '60s in her shop.

4. Brenda goes to yard sales and thrift shops, and she asks friends.

Identify cause and effect.

Sample answers:

1. The causes are that Brenda had a lot of merchandise to sell, and she worked hard to display it.

2. The effect of Brenda working hard on the second sale is that she surprises herself with how well she does.

Use a graphic organizer.

Sample answers:

1. Brenda has a yard sale to sell the stuff.

2. Brenda finds great things to sell.

3. Brenda works hard to find good things for the shop and makes sure people know about it.

Prewriting

The graphic organizer might include the following: her husband suggests a garage sale; Brenda likes the idea; the first sale is a success; Brenda goes to stores and other sales to find good things to sell; the second sale is an even bigger success; Brenda decides to open a vintage shop; she opens Groovy and it is a success.

Thinking Beyond Reading

Answers will vary, but there might now be more items in the graphic organizer.

Write a draft.

Use the details in your chart to help you write.

Revise and create a final draft.

The final draft should include the important events in the story, and the events should be in order. Sentences should be complete and use correct spelling and punctuation.